The Business Owner Defined

A Job Description for the Business Owner

Alexander Visotsky

2015

Visotsky Consulting is a trademark owned by Visotsky Consulting Inc. and used with its permission.

The Business Owner Defined: A Job Description for the Business Owner / Alexander Visotsky. — First edition.

The book was translated by Katya Slepkova. Editing by Jim Wade, Lisa Seplavy, Carol Edwards, Robert Nahas.

ISBN-13: 978-1540422026 (CreateSpace-Assigned)
ISBN-10: 154042202X

CONTENTS

Acknowledgements

This book could not have been written without the support of the employees and partners of Visotsky Consulting, Inc. They are incredibly dedicated to their work and are committed to helping business owners. I want to express special thanks to the business owners who graduated from our Business Owners Program. Many of the ideas for this book came from my conversations with them.

Introduction

One might consider this book to be quite unusual. It is not about how to start a business, or how to earn millions. And it is not for those who dream only about creating their own businesses. Instead, the target reader for this book is someone who has already created his or her own business and continues to participate in the daily activities of the company.

Those who have founded their own businesses often fall into the trap of being too involved in or personally performing the day-to-day operations of the enterprise, only to find they cannot escape — sometimes for a lifetime. They set up companies to achieve their dreams, yet years later they feel like hamsters spinning on a wheel. To some extent, any founder of a company knows that his or her main purpose is not to solve daily operational issues personally. They understand that in focusing on strategic matters, they will be able to contribute much more to the business than by simply making sales or managing technical issues. There is a reason why most small to medium-size business owners cannot escape the daily grind and thus continue to be more like clerks at a grocery store, never «growing out of their first pair of pants.» One might say they become victims of their own success.

People like to continue doing the things about which they feel competent. That makes sense. Success is usually based on a high level of competence, and that includes knowledge, skills, and experience. New companies are created by enthusiasts, the experts in their fields, and it takes years and considerable effort to achieve that high level of excellence in anything. Real pleasure and comfort come only when such competence is acknowledged and results in a loyal client and customer base, an increase in revenues, and public recognition of the brand. It's very rewarding to receive well-deserved recognition. This natural to want to enjoy one's success, but therein lies the trap: There is no desire to change anything fundamentally.

In order for a company founder to rise above day-to-day operational activities, it is necessary to think and act in a completely new way. This means leaving one's familiar comfort zone and going beyond one's current levels of confidence and competence for a period of time. The first step is to figure out in which direction to move, and why. In order to be able to delegate operational management to a top-level executive and become one's own business strategist, it is first necessary to understand what the job is all about.

This book describes the real job of a company owner as a professional activity with certain very precise responsibilities. My intention is to define these responsibilities in a practical and cogent way, since they are actually really simple by nature. While reading this book, you will likely find that you have already been carrying out many of these duties of a business owner intuitively and that all the progress you have made with your business has, in one way or another, been linked to the fact that you have acted in a correct manner. If this were not true, then only graduates of specialized business schools could create successful businesses, and that is not the case. The only difference between a professional approach and an intuitive one is that the professional clearly understands what he or she did right, and what was done incorrectly. Being informed allows for a conscious use of the experience.

I am sure that after reading this book you will have a clearer understanding of the most important duties of a business owner and will be able to do your job in a more informed way. This will give you the opportunity to place operational management into reliable hands and elevate your company to a whole new level.

Chapter 1

The Business Owner's Role

Why do some companies grow large, their names and products familiar to everyone, while others just barely survive, lingering for years on the edge of bankruptcy? For example how was Apple able to create a cult, a fashion, an emotional commitment for its premium-priced products (before 1994, when the iPod and iPhone were not on the market) in a highly competitive market offering products at lower prices? How did they do it? And why is McDonald's so successful? Its restaurants are considered an essential part of any civilized place in the world despite constant criticism by nutrition experts and challenges from competitors. It can be assumed that the reason for success is some amazing product that is available on the market and is so attractive to customers that it guarantees the company a bright future. The product *is* important, but obviously there is something more to it. There are plenty of successful restaurants with delicious food and good service that are not as renowned as McDonald's. Likewise, there are many technological devices, but few are as well recognized as those created by Apple.

You might never have heard of the McDonald brothers' restaurant if one day Ray Kroc, salesman and co-owner of a small company manufacturing mixers for public catering, had not seen a line of customers at the only McDonald's restaurant and gotten excited about the idea of opening a chain of these restaurants based on the same model. Interestingly, Kroc was not the first to franchise the restaurant's operations. The McDonald brothers had been selling franchises for a while without much success. That is why they readily agreed to let Kroc take over the franchise sales.

The point here is that behind every truly successful enterprise there is always a determined individual who is loyal to his own ideals and ready to go all the way. And when such a person is also a very skilled manager, his company achieves unbelievable results. While both the competitive business environment and good market conditions are certainly important, neither are able to create a business masterpiece. Behind every masterpiece, there is always an individual at the top who strategizes everything.

The formation of groups is one of the oldest human endeavors. The history of mankind includes a number of civilizations, but no single civilization could have existed without its founders and leaders. Nowadays, when developed countries choose democracy, this political system seems to enable a group of people to create something worthwhile on their own. But after a more thorough evaluation, it becomes apparent that no single group has achieved considerable success unless that success was purposefully and persistently pursued by the leader of the group. The modern kingdom of corporations, brands, and corporate management creates an illusion that some kind of collective intelligence is responsible for building a successful enterprise. But the fact remains that behind every tremendous success is a talented leader who is loyal to his ideals. Mankind admires this kind of person and remembers his or her name. However, for some strange reason, people try to imitate the external demonstration of success while ignoring its very basis. They focus on the *what*, but give too little consideration to the *why*.

Two Types of Business Owners

In coming to understand the true role of a business owner, it is important to be aware of the two most common types of owners. The ancient works of Indian literature known as the Vedas help give us a way to describe them. Vedic religious traditions, including various characters and philosophic concepts, became a part of such religious and philosophical systems as Brahmanism, Hinduism, Jainism, and Buddhism, all of which were based on the Vedas. The Vedas are a source of socioeconomic and cultural information about ancient Indian history.

According to the Vedas, every person achieves his own level of spiritual development and has the traits and abilities inherent to someone at that level. Ancient Indians called these social levels *varnas*. The Vedas maintained that during his lifetime a person progresses up the levels while forming and developing particular personality characteristics. A person on the highest stage of spiritual personality development is called a Brahmin. Scientists, artists, and religious figures fall into this category. The stage below Brahmin is called Kshatriya. Kings, military commanders, leaders, and all people who devote their lives to service achieve this stage. Then there is the Vaishya stage, mostly represented by merchants and craftsmen. Those at the Vaishya stage can create groups as well, but due to their particular traits, they are fundamentally different from the Kshatriya. The Kshatriya serve their own group and have the group's benefit as their main goal. In contrast, someone at the Vaishya stage needs a group to achieve his own personal success and enrichment. I am not claiming that this classification is very scientific, but it seems to be an apt way to assess different types of leadership. If you study various companies carefully, you will find that particular aspirations and traits inherent to the Kshatriya and the Vaishya are dominant in certain business owners.

A group's achievements depend on its leader. And it is quite valuable to know that any group has a much greater chance of becoming successful if a Kshatriya is the leader, rather than a Vaishya. In contemporary terms, it can be said that a group whose leader does not have a genuine desire to ensure the prosperity of the entire group will never be truly successful. This is not based on conjecture, but on empirical evidence.

In Shanghai, I met the founder, owner, and manager (all one individual) of the B&Y Marketing Agency. At the time, B&Y employed twenty-five people who produced wonderful TV commercials and outdoor advertisements, in addition to designing shopping malls. For the previous few years, the company had stalled out and its yearly revenues had remained at about $1.5 million. I was interested in the discrepancy between the company's high-quality products and its lack of growth, given China's rapid economic development. During my conversation with the owner, I found that his main motive when starting the company was to provide an affluent lifestyle for himself and his family. This business owner was a perfect example of a highly qualified professional Vaishya who was trying to surround himself with assistants just to produce a quality product and enrich himself. It quickly became apparent to me that unless he changed his viewpoint about the way to run his business, his company would never advance.

In 1995, my friends and I started the MacCenter Company in Ukraine. We specialized in selling and servicing Apple computers, and for several years I was the CEO and chairman of the board of directors. Even though the company was relatively small, it was highly professional. Now when I look back, I see that the main reason I founded the company was my personal desire to have a well-paid job that I liked doing.

Like many other enterprises, our company started from nothing. We renovated the office ourselves, tried to get our hands on some affordable office equipment, and had to come up with various schemes to get our first orders. For the first few months, we had to take part-time jobs as security guards because we did not have enough money to pay our staff. We even took turns spending nights at the office, cleaning it, and working as chauffeurs, couriers and porters. At the time, we were not even an authorized Apple reseller and service provider. But we were able to buy a shipment of Macintosh computers from an authorized dealer and, functioning as an intermediary, resell them to another authorized dealer. Our profit from the transactions consisted of two computers, which represented the main «capital» of our company. When we became authorized resellers, our first customers included some Western organizations like Motorola, the U.S. Peace Corps, and USAID, which were just opening offices in Ukraine. We were selling computers to offices and publishing houses, and by the end of our first year, we were the number one reseller in Ukraine. This was the height of our success. We were able to hire a sufficient number of personnel, and we had loyal customers and stable revenues. This was a time when the market was increasing steadily and the opportunities were almost limitless.

However, at the time the company was founded, my partners and I had the motives of a Vaishya—each of us was thinking of increasing personal wealth. That is why, upon achieving some success, the company stopped growing. At the time, I did not realize why that had happened. After operating for three years, I noticed that our competitors had surpassed us, and that it was important for us to expand. But in all of my attempts to reform the company, I encountered resistance from my cofounders. My partners held key executive positions, and as they were satisfied with the company's current level of performance, I was unable to pass my ideas on to them. Neither the other company owners nor I actually understood our functions, nor the tools for growth that were at our disposal. Eventually, after my attempts to turn the situation around were defeated, I left the company. I departed with my chin held high and made a promise to myself: *There is no way in hell I will ever have business partners again.* In that moment, I had not yet realized that it was my own incompetence that was the reason for my failure. One could say that the inner, adventurous Kshatriya had awakened in me, but my own incompetence had led me to defeat.

Since then, I've had many conversations with various company owners and have come to the conclusion that only a small number of them start out as Kshatriyas. Modern culture, at best, aims to raise obedient and hardworking executors, rather than develop leaders. Characteristically, a leader is fanatically loyal to his goals and persistent in their achievement. In his book, *Grinding It Out: The Making of McDonald's*[1], Ray Kroc wrote:

---

[1] Another book about McDonald's I suggest all business owners read is McDonald's: Behind the Arches, by John F. Love (New York: Bantam Books, 1986).

Press On: Nothing in the world can take the place of persistence. Talent will not; nothing is more common than unsuccessful men with talent. Genius will not; unrewarded genius is almost a proverb. Education will not; the world is full of educated derelicts. Persistence and determination alone are omnipotent.

Yet when children are raised in a civilized society, the first thing they learn is to follow the rules. While doing so may make children socially comfortable, it also often suppresses their leadership traits. A child wants to play, but he is forced to go to bed; he wants to get on top of the dresser and jump onto the bed, but his parents don't encourage such acrobatics. Of course, you should not let your children do whatever they want whenever they want—after all, your job is to keep them from harm. But keep in mind that all the behavioral rules imposed by the society, while nurturing, also tend to destroy leadership abilities.

My daughter attended a children's group at a music school, and during one class I noticed a girl who was behaving like a robot. She did everything the instructor asked her to without showing any initiative. Frankly speaking, I felt sorry for her. I realized that this little three-year-old girl had already abandoned all hope of having a say in what happened in the world around her. At the end of class, her mother arrived—the nicest woman in every respect—and, with pleasure, took a seat next to her daughter and started helping the instructor. The way she treated her daughter shocked me. When her daughter dropped a toy she was playing with, she timidly reached out to pick it up. Before she could even finish doing so, her mother told her, «Don't pick it up. Keep playing.» When the girl started playing with a different toy, her mother immediately responded by saying, «Dear, pick up your toys!» And when the girl hesitated a little again, her mother instantly gave her a new instruction: «Sweetie, go dance with the other kids.» Thank God she didn't control her daughter's breathing—it is probably the only reason the girl is still alive! After watching this, my only wish was that the instructor would keep this woman far away from my daughter and the rest of the kids.

It is amazing to me that people raised in a «civilized» and conformist society still aspire to achieve anything. In my opinion, the desire to achieve is the reason many business owners, while in the process of growing their business, go through an evolving set of goals. Starting with the desire to provide themselves and their families with comfortable living conditions, they eventually discover the desire to achieve something more. I am no exception. Having started a business to create a source of income and opportunities for professional growth,

I, too, eventually realized that I wanted to create a really big business game. For whatever reason, it seems that many of us first need to see that we are capable in order to become inspired to create something really worthwhile. From the moment we are born, the world tries to convince us that the only way anybody can become a somebody is by following the rules and being controlled by someone else. It is therefore vital that you come to realize your inner abilities in order to achieve something truly worthwhile.

Take, for example, people who enter the business world right out of school and start successful companies; they all share the same trait. Before going into business, they became experienced and comfortable at managing teams. It's really that simple. A student gets experience as a class president, a member of a student committee, or a project leader; and when the business world becomes accessible, she or he already has a basic understanding of the rules of the game. She knows people need well-defined and achievable goals. She knows people's activities need to be coordinated, and she also knows a great secret: If you tell a person that something needs to be done and that person supports the group's goal, he will do his best to make it happen.

Steve Jobs is an inspiring example of such a group leader. His subordinates claimed that he asked for the impossible—that his standards were too high, and that it was technically impossible to make his dreams come true. The engineers thought Jobs was crazy when he asked them to place the Macintosh LC inside a beautiful but tiny case. When Jobs came up with his legendary Macintosh Classic, he was told that nobody needed such a computer. Jobs pushed his employees to work eighty hours a week and did everything possible to help bring his ideas to fruition. He was so difficult to work with that in 1985 the shareholders decided to oust him. As a protest, Jobs sold all of his shares and started other projects. A series of strategically important mistakes for Apple while under the leadership of a CEO who knew about increasing profits but who operated far from the ideology of the company followed, until Jobs returned in 1996 to rescue a failing company.

In most cases, we need to go through a transformation that helps us realize our abilities, talents, and leadership potential. In fact, a person begins to feel the desire to become stronger than others only when he feels strong enough himself, becomes aware of himself as an individual, and recognizes his talents. That is why when we first start a business and build a team of like-minded people, we experience self-doubt and lack confidence in our abilities. The better our results are, and the more strongly we become convinced of our own abilities, the more evident is the desire to do things that will enhance the lives of other people. Therefore, in building a business, generating some revenues, and building a small team, we get confirmation of our own strength and gain the motivation to grow. So in the business owner is born a Kshatriya.

Chapter 2

....

The First Step to Competency

There is a god I am ready to pray to: the god of competency. Competence is a mixture of knowledge, practical abilities, and creative goals. If one of these elements is lacking, competence does not exist. One can tell whether a person is competent simply by looking at the results of what he has undertaken. If a man is a competent husband and father, his family thrives, his wife is happy, and he is proud of his kids' achievements. If a business owner is competent, his company prospers and grows larger without any headaches. If you are interested in knowing just how competent you are as a business owner, look at your results in this area. If you are always busy with urgent problems, if the company drains your energy and time, then you will never have harmonious operations and growth. Therefore you are currently not competent as a business owner.

You could argue that your company works just fine — better than many others do — and that people even have good reason to be jealous of your achievements. But do not fool yourself. Quite simply, we all have different standards. It doesn't matter what others dream about or what their level of competency is. If instead of working on strategic planning you work on day-to-day problems, and the company's expansion only creates an extra workload for you, then you are not a competent business owner. You may be very good at day-to-day things, but you are not a competent business owner. If you are starting to realize that this is how things are for you, congratulations! You have taken the first step on the path to competence. The first step to competence — although not the easiest — is to admit that there are things you do not understand and that you lack the needed skills and experience. One must admit to a problem before it can be fixed. If a person does not take this step, he will forever be stuck in the mind-set of a know-it-all.

As the result of a merger between two manufacturing companies in 2000, I became a co-owner and CEO of the Geroldmaster Manufacturing

Company[2]. Although at first the company was not the most experienced and well-equipped, by 2004 it had left all of its competitors behind, thanks to the implementation of the management tools discussed in this book. I had no choice but to start this implementation. As the company's production volume had grown larger, the organizational chaos had torn my company apart. Interestingly enough, in spite of all our problems, we were manufacturing the best products. This saved us from alienating and losing customers, even though we were consistently behind schedule.

Once the company was functioning smoothly, I left the CEO position to focus on the owner's role. I started conducting outside seminars on management, during which I explained in detail the organizational know-how that had allowed us to become industry leaders. To my surprise, I found that none of the owners of Geroldmaster's competitors attended my seminars, even though I consistently invited them. It was just unbelievable! Within a few years, Geroldmaster had become the established leader in its field. It was the youngest, most audacious company on the market, with the highest-priced products, which, like a tank, had rolled over the medal-design and -manufacturing industry, making products for government ministries and agencies, the military, and major corporations, as well as for a variety of social and religious organizations. Even though the owners of the competing companies knew that I was providing the answer to the question «How did Geroldmaster do it?» they still did not attend my seminars. They were stuck in an «I know it all» attitude.

When a person is stuck in such a mindset, he has tons of excuses as to why the situation should be exactly as lousy as it is. If you talk with him and ask what the problem is, why things are the way they are, the excuse is «the market conditions,» or «We don't have any experts,» or some other made-up nonsense. But the truth is, that business owner is simply afraid to face the real situation, because upon facing it, he will have to do something that he has probably never done before. He is like a bad driver who blames other drivers, bad road conditions, and the weather. A man with problems in his personal life will tell you what is wrong with modern women and society in general. They simply do not have enough courage to look and see things as they really are.

In order to get rid of this «know it all» attitude, either you need to establish very important goals for yourself, or receive a good kick in

---

[2] Geroldmaster, LLC is a company in Kiev that designs and manufactures souvenirs and medals for various government ministries and agencies, social organizations, and corporations. It also produces military medals. The medals are designed by experienced artists. After a sketch is approved, computer 3-D simulation is done. Complex elements of the medals—portraits, garlands, and the like—are fashioned by sculptors, after which the sculpted models are scanned on a three-dimensional scanner.

the butt. An owner may realize that the results of his hard work are just a weak shadow of the results he desires, or he may find the day-to-day problems become too overwhelming. It is those in the latter group, who want to resolve day-to-day issues, not just cope with them, who most often seek our consulting help.

I wish I could brag that I got out of the «I know it all» attitude thanks to having important goals, but in truth, it was my clients who helped me with this. In 2002, the business was expanding, and as a result we had an almost completely uncontrollable company. Nearly 80 percent of our medal-manufacturing orders were overdue. Since most of our customers were military or government entities, my tenure as CEO was plagued by unpleasant adventures. My workday started and ended with dealing with unhappy customers. There was no way we could even think about strategic planning—I felt as if bullets were whizzing over my head. These unhappy customers were my miraculous kick in the butt. With my feeble attempts to fix things, it took a few months before I realized I had no idea how to run a growing company. That period was a turning point for me. I started looking for answers as to what I should do to make the company more manageable so that I, as the owner, could focus on strategic planning, rather than on fixing small issues.

Unfortunately, not enough literature is available on how well-known companies have handled times like these. The subject of management tools is considered too boring, and often too difficult for most people to comprehend. You can, however, find information on how a particular product was created or how successful manufacturing and retailing companies were started. Interestingly, every prosperous company has its particular management tools, but the general public does not know when and how they were implemented. The reason for this is simple: Only people at the very top of companies are interested in this topic, and their number is limited.

Since you are reading this book, either your goals or your problems have already given you a push, and you are looking for answers to questions related to a business owner's role, as well as to the management of a company. In the following chapters, I will discuss the functions of a Kshatriya in a business, as well as how the business owner's role differs from that of a manager.

Chapter 3

....

The Main Goal and Purpose

The widely known concept of a company mission statement is an essential component of management. It should be noted that this concept can be applied to any group of people, and even to a single person. Various management books give different definitions of the mission statement concept; however, my most precise understanding of it came from studying L. Ron Hubbard's works, particularly the Administrative Scale of a group described in the article «Basic Management Tools»[3]. In the article, he stated that any organization must have an exact and clear main goal and purpose. An effective mission statement is comprised of two parts: the main goal and the purpose. I will discuss this further.

First, however, I want to share my thoughts about Hubbard. I first became acquainted with L. Ron Hubbard's works on management in 1999, and I was surprised to find that in his articles and books he described a set of practical principles that clarifies the foundation for successful management of an organization. The application of these principles in my business yielded excellent results, which enabled us to achieve a new level of expansion for my companies. From 1951 to 1986, Hubbard wrote more than 2,500 articles on various aspects of management, ranging from such topics as rules regarding the relationship between the owner and top executives to the development of marketing strategy and brand positioning. Most of these articles have been published in the nine-volumes The Organization Executive Course. In his articles, Hubbard revealed the laws of «classical management», and he published many noteworthy discoveries in the field of management. To my surprise, these works are not yet widely publicized and few people in the business community have heard about Ron Hubbard as a management expert.

The Main Goal

For the purpose of this discussion, the term *goal* here is not used as more commonly is, as a physical, measurable, achievable thing.

---

[3] L. Ron Hubbard, «Basic Management Tools», in The Management Series, Vol. 2 (Los Angeles: Bridge Publications, 2001), 304.

What is being discussed here is the *main* goal, which is the basis for the ideology of a company, something that makes sense for a group's existence.

During a trip to Novosibirsk, I asked an owner of a construction company, «What is the main goal of your company?» Without any hesitation, he replied, «We work so citizens can admire and be proud of modern Novosibirsk buildings.» His answer surprised and delighted me, since I had gotten used to the state of confusion this question usually triggers. This answer might seem counterintuitive, given that people usually conduct business in order to make a profit. However, the fact is that the main goal of the most popular, successful companies is targeted to benefit a great number of people. It is usually included in the mission statement. For example:

Apple: «To make a contribution to the world by making tools for the mind that advance humankind.»

Google: «to organize the world's information and make it universally accessible and useful.»

Microsoft: «to enable people and businesses throughout the world to realize their full potential.»

McDonald's: «providing outstanding quality, service, cleanliness, and value, so that we make every customer in every restaurant smile.»

It might seem a little strange for people to start businesses if they benefit not just the founders but other people as well. Of course, we all have personal goals in life, things we try to achieve. It can be creative expression, achieving personal comfort, or establishing high living standards for one's family. No matter what your job is, personal goals are equally relevant to a middle manager and to a business owner. One may be dreaming about a sports car, while the other may dream about professional acknowledgment or glory. As a rule the more a person has suffered defeat in the struggle to achieve his goals, the less his desire to achieve goals, and the fewer his personal goals.

When a business owner creates a main goal that does not go beyond his company, but stays «inside,» the company will not be able to expand and overcome obstacles. It is like trying to climb a mountain while having a goal of chatting with friends, or trying to lead an army while having a goal of looking good in a uniform. Of course, this is as silly as it sounds. That is the reason why a main goal «to become number one» inspires only an employee who has self-identification issues, for it is vitally important to such an individual to stand out from the crowd, and being an employee of a number-one company is a way of achieving this. But what does this have to do with the main goal of the group? Such a goal would be boring to people with high self-esteem who want to achieve big goals. It doesn't mean that «becoming number one» is a bad goal; it just cannot be the main goal. It is a good mid-level goal on the way to achieving something more. It is impossible to expand your influence without breaking out of your shell, working only in perfect comfort and coziness inside. I will discuss mid-level goals at greater length in chapter 12.

The main goal is relatively simple, as truth is simple. Fools are fools only because they cannot accept the truth as it is. Therefore, to perceive something closer to the truth, such people need to add some form of complexity. Only then will they look at the complexity, wrinkle their brows, and discuss it. For example, when somebody says that his personal goal is, «to increase people's abilities,» others might ask, «What for? What is the sense?» The silliness of these questions is that the goal, on its own, is the basis for the sense. There is no clearer sense than this for the basis of the goal. What is the sense in climbing mountains, or what is the sense of competing in a contest, other than reaching the summit or triumphing in competition? Do not look for any clearer sense to a main goal than the intention to achieve that goal.

This is what the Grundfos Corporation says about their main goal: «It is our mission — the basis of our existence — to successfully develop, produce and sell high-quality pumps and pumping systems world-wide, contributing to a better quality of life and a healthy environment.» Do you see? The company aspires to achieve its main goal of «contributing to a better quality of life and a healthy environment» while producing pumps. Certainly if the water-supply and sewage-removal systems in your house work well, then the quality of your life is better. Why, exactly, is Grundfos's goal worded as it is? Simply because this idea came to the company founder's mind and he had the authority to make it so. There is no other reason. Why does Apple declare that its goal is «to make a contribution to the world by making tools for the mind that advance humankind.»? Because Steve Jobs decided so. Why does McDonald's say its goal is «to make every customer in every restaurant smile»? Because Ray Kroc decided so. These main goals are not necessarily unique. Without working hard to achieve them, they would never be a key to a successful company. These goals create long-term meaning for such companies and provide clarity about what is good and what is bad, what is right and what is wrong.

A company's main goal does not need to be absolutely unique. Its purpose is usually more distinctive. Just like Grundfos strives to improve the quality of peoples' lives, thousands of other companies and organizations seek to achieve a similar goal. This, on its own, does not weaken a company's employees' aspirations to reach that goal. While Visotsky Consulting helps to turn businesses around by implementing management tools targeted to improve a company's management culture and enhance its effectiveness, thousands of other consulting and business-training companies seek to achieve this same goal. However, a company's purpose is always individual.

The Purpose

The second part of a mission statement is to define the company's purpose. Every strong company has its own individual operating style, which determines the actions of that company. For example, Apple's purpose is to develop both software and hardware to achieve ideal compatibility with one another. Unlike Microsoft's operating system, Apple's OS and certain applications were designed to work only on Apple hardware. Apple was a total and self-contained package. In 1995, before Steve Jobs returned to the company, Apple's management decided to change this purpose and sold the license to manufacture Apple-compatible computers (using Apple's OS) to a few companies, most notably to Motorola and Power Computing. Apple then had to suffer the consequences. Abolition of third-party manufacturer licensing was one of the first things Jobs did upon his return to the company. If the main goal determines the general orientation of the company's operations, the purpose determines a specific, particular way of operating that the group is trying to achieve. It may sound complicated, but in essence, it is very simple.

Let's look again at the Grundfos mission statement. Its first part, «to successfully develop, produce, and sell high-quality pumps and pumping systems worldwide», is actually a pretty clear purpose statement. It is how they are going about fulfilling the main goal of «contributing to a better quality of life and a healthy environment.» By the way, Apple has another purpose, which Steve Jobs always carried out well: The products have to be aesthetically pleasing. In fact, the design is even more important than the technical elements in manufacturing. The design of every aspect of the visible and user-function controls and ports was just as important as the technology operating inside. If Apple remains loyal to this purpose, it will never manufacture cheap products, as the low cost of such products is achieved by improving the internal technological process at the expense of slick design and user-friendly interfaces. As for McDonald's, the main part of their purpose is cleanliness, a limited number of items on the menu, and fast service. By stating its purpose, the company's owner predetermines what the company is going to be like. For example,

Visotsky Consulting's purpose is consulting with business owners and leading them through the difficulties of implementing essential management tools. Our purpose is embodied in our core product, the Business Owners Program. We do not do anything else.

It is important to focus on defining the organization's purpose, as this is what will lead the group to fulfilling its main goal. If a small company has too broad a purpose, it will just waste its resources. If instead the purpose is more narrowly defined, the company will concentrate its resources toward its main goal. Take, for example, a furniture manufacturer that defines as its main goal «creating comfort in life,» and its purpose as «to design, manufacture, and sell modern, well-designed furniture made available to a wide range of customers.» The intent is very well defined. Clearly, the manufacturer will not produce luxury furniture and will not use high-grade natural wood. A well-defined purpose determines which market a company will serve, who its customers will be, its distribution process, and which resources and equipment it will use.

In 2003, my business partner and I formulated one of the purposes of the Geroldmaster Company — namely, «to produce medals that perfectly match their designers' creative ideas while prioritizing quality over the manufacturing process.» It may seem a strange purpose for a manufacturing company, but that is how it was stated at the outset. The fact is, the company started with just a small office specializing in medal design. It was founded by designers who had a pretty good but, as it later turned out, naïve idea. They saw the medals that Ukraine received from the USSR and decided to design more inspiring ones. The underlying idea was «to design and fulfill manufacturing orders using already existing facilities,» but the idea contained the above-mentioned purpose. When the first orders of Jubilee Awards for the State Corporation for the Production of Armaments and the Emeritus Employee of the Tax Service medals were designed and manufactured, two things became clear. First, the existing manufacturing facilities could only produce products at the prior level of quality, rather than improved, value-added quality. Second, these manufacturing facilities could only produce the products they had been producing for years, since the idea of making the processes faster and cheaper had been the most important standards to follow. It was impossible to implement Geroldmaster's purpose with this approach. That was the reason that, over time, the design office eventually turned into a manufacturing facility with a unique production cycle of models and molds for manufacturing medals. The unique part was that when the customer approved a medal design, special software allowed all of the geometrically correct elements of the medal to be modeled, directly based on the approved design. If the medal contained a wreath, figures, or any reliefs, their prototypes were hand-sculpted first. Next, a 3-D scan was performed, the model was finished on the computer, and special equipment transferred the computer model into a metal one. As far as I know, to this day it is the only facility with such fast and perfect manufacturing tooling technology. The creation of such a process was not just the owners' whim. All we wanted to do was accomplish the main purpose: to make sure the manufactured medals matched the intended design. It was simple, made sense, and proved to be commercially successful. Despite fairly high prices, our customers came back to us time and again. None of our competitors could match the same level of quality, and with regard to medals, people were not willing to compromise quality in order to save money. I am not saying there were no customers who prioritized price; they just weren't Geroldmaster's customers. This is neither good nor bad, as it is impossible to satisfy everybody's needs: those who want well made products and those who want cheap ones. That is why companies with different purposes are needed. In the end, there will always be a Mercedes and there will always be a KIA. Such companies have different purposes and, accordingly, different customers.

Incidentally, when a business is just getting started, there is always some new purpose being formed—for example, «We repair used Japanese cars,» or «We bake confectionary products according to local customers' tastes.» These are not the most ideal purpose statements. The more specific a purpose is, the stronger it is. One could say that, ideally, the intent should have some unique element that provides a competitive advantage.

Preserving the purpose and making sure the company does not deviate from it is not an easy job. In Visotsky Consulting's company, our customers, consultants, and business owners promote some new idea every month. Our purpose was precisely formulated for such a reason. Before this actively expanding company was started, I had the usual consulting projects. I found companies and then worked with the owners or managers under contract. I, along with some assistants, implemented the management tools and left when the job was done. However, I found this was not a good approach, for two reasons. First, during such projects, you cannot pay enough attention to improving the competence of the owner. His 100 percent understanding of how the management tools work determines whether these tools will really be applied in the company. Second, when the consultant turns the company around, he, in fact, takes on the authority, becoming the employees' boss. But this completely contradicts the idea that is the main goal of our company, which is to help business owners become stronger. I was able to turn the situation around when I came up with a way to implement the management tools with the owners' own hands. In essence, this is the purpose of our company. And it looks like we are the only ones who do not do the owners' job for them, but instead help them to do it themselves. That is why proposals to teach the clients' personnel instead of directly focusing on the business owners go against the purpose of our company. Such ideas will never be implemented. On the other hand, any proposals that contribute to our main purpose and help business owners become stronger, I will consider with interest. And if I see that they truly align with our main purpose, I will gladly implement them.

Between the years 1990 and 2000, there were many Ukrainian companies that are examples of companies without a clear purpose. Their sole purpose was to make money, and this, in fact, is simply a lack of clear purpose. Naturally, such companies jumped on every opportunity to make money and introduced a variety of services. In remote areas, there are still companies that do general wholesale, retail, catering, et cetera. And now when narrowly specialized companies come into these areas and start operating, they successfully push the locals out of business. How should the local companies deal with these specialized companies? They first need to realize that a multioperational company is, essentially, a set of groups — a complex of companies within itself, every one of which has its own main goal and purpose. Managing these subsidiaries means managing every single company separately, as they indeed are separate businesses. I will discuss this further in my next book about business structure and functions.

If you read the mission statements of different companies and analyze their operations, you will find that every strong business has a distinct purpose. Very often, that purpose involves some know-how. To John D. Rockefeller, the purpose was merging small oil-producing and refining companies through stock purchases in exchange for shares in the merged Standard Oil Company. This purpose very quickly led to his control of the entire industry. Moreover, he gained total control of the transportation of oil from the wellhead to the refinery and distribution beyond, thereby enabling himself to set prices that forced producers either to be absorbed by Standard Oil or to go out of business.

While highly successful in this goal, his monopoly of the process from production through transport and refining to retail sale led to the antitrust breakup of Standard Oil. Note that there are no absolute decisions, one being the best over all others. Any purpose is successful to some degree, and to some degree it creates a weakness. For example, Steve Jobs's refusal to sell licenses for Apple's operating system resulted in Microsoft's complete domination of the operating systems market. Every personal computer manufacturer used the Windows operating system and more than a few software developers produced versions compatible only with the Microsoft system. On the other hand, this same purpose by Apple helped create the most convenient computer platform, which is just a pleasure to work with. Those who have used Apple computers do not usually switch to Windows unless they are forced to by some specific circumstance. The almost cultlike loyalty of Apple computer users provided a critical base of early adopters of the iPod, the iPod touch, and all the subsequent products — users who spread word-of-mouth testimony and enthusiasm that supercharged Apple's launches and incredible growth in unit sales (at premium prices).

When formulating purposes, it is important to take three things into consideration. First, there are products (merchandise or services) that potential customers are ready to pay for, and there are those for which they are not. For example, what can be more important than preschool education for children? Whether a child will be creative, whether he will want to learn and apply his knowledge, and what his values will be all fully depend upon the way he is treated during his preschool years. Essentially, his future, the future of those around him, and that of all mankind will be determined during this time. You would think providing preschool education would be a priceless service, right? But the truth is, for some strange reason many people believe that anyone can take care of children, and therefore they do not like to pay for it. The idea of paying a thousand dollars a month for a child's preschool seems crazy to some parents, even when that parent is driving an eighty thousand dollars car! There is nothing rational about it. In five years, that piece of metal will not be worth even half of what it cost, and eventually it will fall apart completely. But try to open a kindergarten where kids are taken care of by caring and highly qualified professionals and charge a reasonable price, and you will see that a purpose like this is difficult to bring to life. By the way, start-ups with uncommon purposes very often fail not because they don't benefit the consumer, but because their purposes are too complicated for most of their potential customers to understand and recognize their benefits. Tremendous effort is required to convey the benefits to them, which is not an easy job for a small company.

Second, in formulating a purpose, you must consider whether it is possible to make the purpose generate large-scale activity. For example, you have a talented craftsman who can create amazing leather bindings for books. A good book with a leather binding could be a wonderful present for any serious reader. You could sell this product all over the world. But there is the question of whether it is possible to create a whole army of such craftsmen and whether it is possible to teach a number of people to create such bindings with the same degree of skill. Also, is there equipment that would allow you to produce the bindings in sufficient quantity? Hamburgers and fries are not difficult to make, yet Ray Kroc still had to open Hamburger University so that those operating his franchisees could do a quality job. IKEA is another great example. That company's purpose becomes clear if you read a book about its founder, Ingvar Kamprad, entitled *Leading by Design: The Ikea Story*. I remember one story from the book in which Ingvar was in one of Ikea's competitor's stores and saw a drinking glass that was in high demand at the time. He went to his purchasing manager and asked whether it was possible to get the same glasses for a significantly lower price. The manager collected the necessary information and later replied that it was possible to get it much cheaper, but Ikea would have to sell over a million of such glasses. Ingvar gladly accepted the deal and, as a result, the glass was a best-seller, bringing the company good revenues.

Usually we say that a business's purpose is successful if it allows the company to expand significantly. Expansion requires energy — that is, money — and you can only get a lot of this energy if you provide customers with high volumes of your product. For this reason, companies that make their expertise available to only a limited number of customers never become large and thriving businesses. For example, I like to educate business owners on the subject of strategy, but I do not know how to teach other consultants to do it with the same success. Because I cannot put this product on a «production line,» I would not start a company with the purpose of providing customers with these particular consulting services.

Third, the purpose must provide a company with an advantage over its competitors. For example, McDonald's purpose is «fast customer service,» which is why, even with relatively low prices, the restaurants can afford to be located in buildings and shops in the most highly trafficked areas, have good-quality kitchen equipment, and still retain their high profit margin. Starbucks's purpose is to provide the highest-quality coffee; it started as a coffee supplier to various coffee shops and restaurants. Now there are more than seventeen thousand stores operating under the Starbucks name. Starbucks is active in preserving its purpose, which I personally witnessed while visiting their stores in various countries. Without such a purpose, the company would never have been able to retain its quality standards and would not have gained the well-deserved recognition of its customers.

Apple products are always distinguished by their reliability and user-friendliness, thanks to the company's purpose to develop both the hardware and software themselves. Nobody else in the world has an opportunity to create a similar computer product. Developers of other operating systems are forced to make them versatile so they will run on all types of computers. Hardware manufacturers have to consider the capabilities of these other operating systems. Only Apple can afford to create revolutionary technologies of such quality and with such speed, and this has turned out to be a huge advantage for Apple in the personal computer industry. While Apple still produces and markets desktops and laptops, which are available through resellers and its own many retail stores and the online Apple Store, its greatest volume (unit sales) is accounted for by the iPhone and the iPad.

Thus, a successful purpose must take into consideration the market conditions and potential customers' viewpoint, existing technology and resources, and an idea that provides a competitive advantage. But there is one more important point. This purpose should reflect the fundamental idea and personality of its founder. In modern society, individuality is valued at a premium. Just consider those professionals who are the highest-paid and get the most publicity. These include certain actors and performers of popular music, writers, scientists, and sports figures. They are either people who have enough courage to show a personal point of view in what they create, or those who have transformed themselves into a product—a pop-culture idol like Miley Cyrus or Beyonce. In a 2010 rating of the most popular people, the first ten positions were taken by such performers and sports figures. These are people who promote their personality traits and talents to the whole world. In our society, things that are considered to be rare become expensive. Why do marketing gurus such as Jack Trout command tens of thousands of dollars per presentation? You don't think it's because of the great practical value of the information, do you? You can get significantly more information if you read Trout's books on marketing and branding. People are eager to touch the revered and profound person who is courageous enough to express his or her opinion during a time when most of the people on this planet deny the very ability to have a point of view of their own. On the one hand, they deny it in themselves, and on the other, they admire it in others. It is not difficult to see that the magically alluring trait that everyone calls charisma is nothing more than the courage to express a personal point of view. Having charisma does not mean people will necessarily agree with you. It is the courage to have and express a personal opinion that attracts people.

When it comes to leadership, the foundation is very simple. A leader is a person who has found enough courage and persistence to set a main goal and purpose for a group. It is that simple: courage and persistence. Notice that I did not say anything about intelligence. It is desirable but not vital. If this seems incredible to you, just listen to the majority of political leaders who are followed by millions of people and you will be able to see for yourself. When we were kids, we would meet our friends after school in the school yard and then wander from corner to corner, suffering from idleness until someone suggested, «Let's build a fort», «Let's play soccer,» or some other activity. If the boy who made the suggestion was able to advance his idea and get others to be in favor of it, then he would become the leader at that particular time. We then had a very meaningful (at least *we* thought so) activity to engage in, and our game began. Any game was better than no game, and any leader was better than no leader.

From the viewpoint of experience, we could debate the purposefulness of such games, but boys who wander around aimlessly are happy to engage in any activity. Modern culture often offers people very boring games: wrapping your body in a fashionably branded piece of cloth, buying a shiny car to take you places quickly, and building a house with thick walls. But the most talented people, even if they cannot dream of something really large, respond to an interesting or challenging game offered, even if it goes beyond their usual daily routines. If you create an important goal and attractive purpose, it inspires those who still have a taste for life.

The first role of a business owner is to create an inspiring main goal and a clearly defined purpose. It is the very first thing you need to do, no matter whether you've already started out on your journey as a Vaishya or you are one of those rare people who have survived the civilized world as a Kshatriya.

Chapter 4

....

A Business Owner's Personal Goals

A business owner, along with all other company employees, is, of course, part of a group. Every group member fulfills his own particular responsibility as a salesperson, an accountant, a process engineer, et cetera. An organization is a system whose members perform specific functions. A salesperson works with customers; an accountant handles financial transactions and maintains records; an engineer develops new processes and monitors their compliance. In this system, the owner plays a special role. His function is to establish goals that will unite the entire group. But in this capacity, he may encounter a trap that is easy to fall into.

As I discussed in the previous chapter, every person has his or her own individual goals. Only people completely disappointed in life do not have goals. Every salesperson and accountant dreams of a new house, a car, a cruise, a special gift for a loved one, and a business owner is no exception. Just like the others, he has his own personal goals that he dreams of achieving. He dreams about amassing personal wealth, about houses and cars, about comfort and vacations, and about opportunities to do something creative. There are as many goals as there are different kinds of people. And the more capable a person is, the more individualistic his or her aspirations will be.

At the same time, the owner is the only person in the company who is responsible for establishing goals for the entire group. He is the only one whose function it is to establish these goals, and then direct the group's attention to them. That is where the catch is. The owner can confuse his or her personal goals and dreams with the business's goals and purposes.

Interacting with many business owners, I occasionally meet people who say, «The goal of my company is to make money, increase assets and the company's market value.» These people have no idea that they are not talking about the company's goals, but about their personal ones. The owner has a goal of increasing the company's value and wants his or her «baby» to continually grow. This point of view could be compared to that of a father who wants his child's only goal to be to serve his parent. This is a completely unnatural point of view.

Of course, a child should bring his parents joy, but it should be the joy of his own successes, achievements, and victories on the way to his individual goals. When the owner of a company says that the company's goal is «to increase the company's value,» he really means, «My goal is to become rich.» He is not talking about the group's goal, but about his personal one. A group's goal cannot be someone's dream of becoming happy and rich.

Once, during a workshop, the owner of a roofing materials manufacturing and retailing business approached me. His company employed around fifty people. They manufactured copper shingles, gutters, and other parts for copper roofing. Our conversation went as follows.

«Our company manufactures a good product and our customers are happy. It is certainly not a cheap product, but the customers who know us usually thank us for our services. But there's one issue I still can't understand. When I start my workday, I'm full of energy. I meet with the customers and manage my employees. The window of my office faces the sales department, and since I usually arrive at the office earlier than everybody else, I get to observe my employees as they come in. You know, we try to take care of our employees. Their salaries are high and the working conditions are good, but when they get to work, they look like they have been working hard all night long and can't wait to finally get some rest. They barely move. And unless they get enough coffee, they cannot even start working. Why is it this way? I am full of energy and desire to work, but why aren't they?»

«What is the main goal of your business?» I asked him.

«What goal? It is to make money for me, of course!»

«Imagine you just joined a good company as a salesperson. During the orientation period, you are told, «The goal of our company is to make another million dollars for the owner!» Would that inspire you?»

«No. I get it,» he said after giving it some thought.

When the company owner confuses his personal goals with the goals of the company, he creates goals for the company that do not motivate his employees. Imagine a company where during corporate events it is announced, «Our goal is to make our owner rich!» It doesn't seem as if anyone would honestly want to put any effort into achieving this goal. Only when employees want to achieve the company's goals will you see the spark in their eyes and will they be full of energy and creativity. This does not mean that when you establish goals for the entire group that you must renounce your personal goals. Giving up your own goals can lead to a complete lack of joy and pleasure for you. I personally think that a miserable person will not be able to be particularly useful to other people. Keep your goals. Just take care not to confuse them with the goals you establish for your company.

Think big. Don't waste your time on pseudogoals like «making more money,» «benefiting everybody,» or even «becoming number one in the industry.» Assess what the company can realistically achieve in the long run. If you manufacture furniture, maybe your goal would be «providing comfort and design for people's lives.» If you are a grocery wholesaler, perhaps it would be «creating high-quality living standards for a wide range of people by providing a fresh and premium-quality range of grocery items.» Of course, these goals need to reflect your own aspirations and talents. One owner will start a company to bring the latest technology to the market. Another owner will start a company to provide satisfying and cheerful service. Ever since he started walking, my nephew, Vasiliy, has amazed the people around him with one particular habit: He cannot walk past an excavator, truck, crane, or tractor without stopping to admire it. The boy can just stand there and admire such machines, enjoying them. As you can imagine, his mother does not share his fascination, and every time he stops to gaze, she tries to pull him away. What kind of company will he start when he grows up? I don't know, but I do know one thing for sure: If he does become an owner of company that a produces construction machinery, he will be doing what he likes most. What goals will he establish for the company? Perhaps they will be «to provide construction workers with reliable and efficient machinery and contribute to the prosperity of the construction industry.» Companies' goals are really very distinct, as individual as their owners.

Trying to set up a goal based on the individual goals of the group members is also a common mistake made by business owners. The owner needs to be aware that as the founder as well as a member of the group, he performs a very specific function: He forms the goal for the entire group. An example of this kind of mistake would be to say, «Our company's goal is to provide customers with a quality product, increase owners' equity, and create a decent standard of living for our employees.» This is not a goal. It is merely an attempt to please everyone who has something to do with the company — employees, owners, and customers. And this attempt to please is the exact opposite of the manifestation of individuality. A problem with such goal formation is that people are not so naïve as to believe that this is really the group's goal.

I am genuinely surprised by what results when some not very clever consultants' brainstorm about the main goal and purpose of a company with its top management team. They come up with these monstrous ideas that do not inspire anyone—not managers, owners, or employees. Have some fun by reading the goals and mission statements of some of these various companies online.

Occasionally, I help owners to create mission statements for their companies. I first ask them questions that relate to the purpose of the company. I ask what the initial business idea was and whether it had any competitive advantage that distinguished the company from its competitors. I ask the owner to describe the company's operations in a few words. When the purpose is clear, I help him or her state the main goal by asking questions about what would change in the company's external environment if it successfully carried out its purpose. Why do I start with the purpose? I do this because the purpose is more concrete to people, as it will determine the company's course of action. The main goal, however, is less apparent, though in essence it is predetermined by the purpose.

When you create the main goal of the group, don't think about whether employees will like it. The most important thing it should do is inspire. Look around at the leaders of some outstanding companies. As a rule, they dedicate their whole lives to doing their favorite job. They have enough courage to do what inspires them. And they create main goals that attract the right people to their companies and encourage them to stay.

Chapter 5

The Pursuit of Money

The business world is brainwashed by the idea that the goal of any business is to make money. Of course, the people who made this idea popular are not very smart; they do not understand anything about money at all. Money is just a medium of exchange. The amount of money a company makes depends on how useful its products or services are, and how widely available these products or services are. Behind every product, there is a particular person's dream, as well as a goal that inspires an entire team to overcome any obstacles along the way to creating the product. Long before Mark Zuckerberg became a billionaire, he refused Microsoft's generous offer to buy the program he'd developed. The reason was simple. When he came up with the idea of Facebook, he was thinking about creating a communication and social-networking platform for university students, not about columns of numbers on a financial statement.

Making lots of money is a great idea, but in reality, the meaning behind business is to create a lot of something that people will consider useful and want to obtain. The main goal of a company should be an exact wording of this aspiration, not the expression of a desire to receive as much money as possible.

«I want to work for a company that contributes to and is part of the community. I want something not just to invest in. I want something to believe in.» — Anita Roddick, The Body Shop

Of course, you do not get paid for your aspirations alone, and rarely do aspirations without tangible results receive support. However, to say that the main goal of a business is to make profits is the same as saying that the goal of a human is to breathe. Without being able to breathe, a person cannot survive for long, because breathing is essential for a person to move, think, and create. Every person has his or her own main goal. Some dream about teaching children, others dream of constructing beautiful buildings, and still others desire to raise talented and independent children. Without breathing for more than just a few minutes, a person would not be able to achieve any of these goals. This is comparable to the important role of money for a business or any other organization.

«Money is like gasoline during a road trip. You don't want to run out of gas on your trip, but you're not doing a tour of gas stations.» — Tim O'Reilly, O'Reilly Media founder and CEO

Any good idea can be brought to the point of absurdity. For example, since ancient times there have been practices in which followers try to improve themselves with sophisticated ways of breathing. Likewise, there are business practices that claim that proper money handling and money management are the keys to success. This is only partly true. It is really important to handle money wisely, but good money management alone does not lead to success. That is because money management is simply a tool for managing the exchange process of your product for money.

Increased profits and growth of gross income can be wonderful mid-level goals and important milestones in a company's growth, but they are never main goals that can lead you to victory. Only a person who has completely lost his or her ideals sees personal needs as the only reason for owning a business and can accept making money as its main goal. Such an viewpoint is acceptable for an unskilled worker, but is not acceptable for someone who has started a company.

Chapter 6

....

Motivation

You have probably noticed that people have various levels of motivation with respect to their work. Some begin work with enthusiasm, but for others, it takes a great deal of effort to make them work, even under the constant supervision of a superior. Some are really interested in their jobs, yet others see their job simply as a harsh necessity. It is all about motivation. In modern society, *motivation* can mean a person's desire to work, the actions a manager performs to achieve results, or even a company's wage system. In its simplest terms, the word *motivation* is defined as an impulse that propels a person toward some activity. *Motivation* comes from the word *motive*, which means «an incentive, purpose, or reason for some action.» *Motive*, in turn, comes from the Latin word *movēre*, which means «to move.» Thus motivation is something that makes people move in some area of activity.

While managing companies, I noticed that there are those who are dedicated to their jobs, and those who are free riders, who are willing to go along for the ride as long as someone else does the driving. It is pretty easy to deal with the first type of person. She is loyal to the company and produces, to the extent of her competency, good results. To put it simply, these are people you can rely on. When there is a need to solve urgent problems, you call upon these individuals to obtain the needed support. L. Ron Hubbard provided a good classification of different levels of motivation[4]. He described four main levels of motivation, from highest to lowest:

- Duty
- Personal Conviction
- Personal Gain
- Money

Duty

The highest motivation level is duty. On this level, people consider a company they work for to be part of their lives. They are loyal to

---

[4] L. Ron Hubbard «Promotion and Motivation», in The Organization Executive Course: Public Division, vol. 6 (Los Angeles: Bridge Publications, 1991), 158.

the company and its interests. They are reliable and give support to managers. There may be many people working for a company, but rarely are the majority those with a duty level of motivation.

Personal Conviction

People who are not company patriots but consider themselves professionals and try to do their jobs well according to their personal standards of professionalism are people on the personal conviction level of motivation. For example, this could be an accountant who does not care what the company does or how well it succeeds, but by virtue of personal conviction, thinks it is important to ensure that the accounting department is run properly.

Personal Gain

The next level of motivation is personal gain. People on this level do their jobs just to get some benefits from the company. These benefits range from the intangible, such as experience, knowledge, and networking, to the tangible, such as the company's convenient location, compensation, and other benefits. These people often tell you that they are ready to deliver fantastic results if you provide higher pay and better benefits. Sometimes they sound very convincing. If you have ever gone along with this kind of person's plea, then you know it does not work. Their level of production does not increase in proportion to their appetite.

Money

The last level of motivation is money, and it is actually pretty rare to find a person at this level, as this is a level of motivation in which, strictly speaking, a person does not even care what he does as long as he makes more money doing it. Although many people say they are interested only in money, this is not actually true. Just try offering an engineer who constantly complains about being underpaid a better-paying job as sales manager. Typically, he would tell you that he wants to work in his specialty. This means that his level of motivation is not money, but personal conviction. People who are on the money level of motivation usually have some serious money troubles and are ready to do anything possible to solve them.

It should be noted that the higher levels of motivation are accompanied by the lower ones. Thus a person on the level of duty is also motivated by the personal conviction, personal gain, and money levels. The fact that he has a duty level of motivation does not mean he would not be interested in money. Money is just not the first priority. When he acts, he thinks first about the company, and only then does he consider the reward he might get. This is why you should be careful not to stigmatize somebody who asks for a raise. Such a request does not necessarily mean that money is the person's main motivation. In order to determine the person's true motivation, you should look at what drives him when he does his job, not concentrate on whether he asks for more money.

A person on the personal conviction level of motivation acts according to his or her own beliefs about what is right and wrong. Of course, he also operates on the personal gain and money motivation levels, but not on the level of duty motivation. With this type of person, as long as his or her principles and views correspond with the company's goals, there are no problems. However, if in order to achieve the company's goals you have to ask for something from him that does not agree with his beliefs about what is right and wrong, you will face problems in managing this kind of person. For example, say that you hired a new chief accountant who is functioning on the personal conviction level of motivation, and his conviction is that the accounting department should be perfectly in order. He has his own idea about what «perfectly in order» means. You are happy about finding such a great person because your idea about how an accounting department should function means not having any problems with the IRS. As time goes by and your company becomes more structured, you notice that the accounting department slows down the company's work flow. For example, it takes too long to get some orders written and to account for financial transactions. You decide to change the work procedures in the accounting department and find that your chief accountant, who completely supported all of your ideas before and seemed very professional to you, all of a sudden starts working against your ideas and creating problems. The reason for this is simple. He operates on the personal conviction level of motivation and is not motivated to work in the company's best interest, but, rather, in accordance with his own principles.

In the middle of this incentive scale, one can arbitrarily draw a line between the personal conviction and personal gain levels. Above this line are people who try to do their jobs well because of their own personal desire. They are the most dedicated to their jobs. Below the line are people who, upon receiving their position in the company, focus not on how to get the job done, but on what they need to do, if anything, to receive their desired benefits. It is pretty easy to manage the two types above the arbitrary line, as they are focused on getting the job done. It is more difficult to manage the two types below the line because you have to deal with their constant calculations regarding their personal gain. When it comes to salaries, different approaches are required here. Any fair pay system suits people with a high motivation level, as they work without thinking about money. For people with a low motivation level, the pay system should be such that it encourages and rewards every correct action and penalizes every wrong one.

Interestingly, people have different levels of motivation in different areas of their lives. For example, there are many who have a duty level of motivation toward their family, and a personal gain level toward their job. You hire such a person and think, *If he is so proud of his kids and takes such good care of his family, he will definitely be a good employee!* But, in reality, there is no connection between the two. I have met several fathers who were loyal to their families but who could not be forced to work, even with a stick. This becomes clear when you understand how to gauge a persons level of motivation correctly.

Consider a very large group, such as the population of a country. If you traced how the average level of motivation of the Soviet people changed over time, you would find that the highest increase in motivation was during and right after World War II. According to statistics, during the war it was unusual for soldiers to get sick from common diseases, even though the living conditions were deplorable. The highest level of patriotism was also during and immediately following the war. The lowest level of motivation was right after the collapse of the USSR. The reason for this was the motivation itself. If a person accepts the goals of a group as his own, he is at the level of duty. The goals of the country during and after the war were clear and important to the majority of the people. Due to explicit threats and efficient propaganda, almost everyone understood that there was a simple goal during the war: to defeat the enemy; after the war, it was to restore the economy. After the collapse of the USSR, all the goals that the ruling party had directed people toward for decades through the use of propaganda were destroyed, but new ones had not yet been established. This is why the country experienced a period of the lowest motivation in the entire history of the Soviet Union. The country was effectively pulled to pieces. Do not think that I sympathize with the Communists. I do not. However, their use of management tools — namely, setting goals, then skillfully and persistently promoting those goals of unifying the Soviet Union in the face of mortal threat — has to be commended. During Soviet times, goal-oriented propaganda penetrated so deeply into all aspects of society that even a university thesis on mechanical engineering could not be successfully defended without discussing the role of the next Party Congress in the manufacturing of hubs and cogwheels.

Perhaps this is the biggest secret of leadership: In order to create and support high levels of motivation, it is necessary for people to share the goals of the group. If the leader is skilled enough to form and promote goals, he will be surrounded by people with high levels of motivation. Promotion of goals is the most important tool for creating such levels of motivation, and goal promotion plays an important role in groups with the highest levels of motivation. Goal promotion is a set of actions that conveys to a group some ideas in order to form a particular point of view.

If you observe, you will find that there are companies where people work with enthusiasm, and there are companies where all the employees remain on no more than the personal gain level of motivation. Most commonly, within a company there is a small group of highly motivated people, and then there are the rest. As a rule, this small group consists of people who have been working side by side with the leader for a long time. Perhaps these are the people who have worked for the company since it first started. However, newer employees do not have such motivation. The reason for this is that when the company first started, the owner attracted people who shared his goals and intentions and agreed with his vision of the future. He was likely low on funds, and intuitively relied on the most powerful of tools: goals. As time passed, the company learned to produce a product and make money, and goal promotion was replaced with «solid» incentives such as salaries, stability, and career-advancement opportunities. The most important tool for establishing motivation was abandoned and forgotten. Moreover, the company grew relatively large, and personal communication with the owner became available only to those who were within his inner circle in the company.

It is important to realize that the promotion of goals and ideals should be pursued continuously from the moment a company is established. If the owner in the above example had continued promoting goals and purposes and informing each employee about them even after the company grew large, then the number of people with a high level of motivation would have increased proportionally with the company's growth. When one hires people, the most important thing one wants from them is their creative energy, not just their muscle power or obedience in following orders and policies. In order for that to happen, it is important to raise their level of motivation. It is obvious that when a new employee joins a company, he is either functioning on the personal conviction or personal gain level. In order to raise his level of motivation to duty, it is important for the leader to fulfill his mission and inspire an employee with the goals of the group.

In modern society, the idea that it is important to provide people with goals that are clear and relevant to them in order to motivate them is very popular. One popular idea is that if you want to motivate a person who wants to build a house or buy a car, you must show him that the goals of the company are related to his personal goals. In my opinion, this is a vulgar and completely useless idea. Such ideas are furthered by those who consider adaptation the only means of survival. However, strong groups do not adapt. Strong leaders do not conform. They adjust the environment to fit their goals. Whom did Steve Jobs conform to when he invited only the best computer geeks to join his team? No one. He simply promoted the goals of the company to the finest computer specialists, then provided them with the opportunity to create outstanding products and work in an atmosphere with the most talented people. That is why the best engineers and developers joined his company. In spite of his bad temper, they were ready to work eighty hours a week to create outstanding products. A leader cannot increase a person's motivation by trying to adapt to his or her personal goals.

Some people are readily inspired by the goals of a group, while others never progress higher than the personal gain level of motivation. During one of my workshops on motivation, someone offered up the following idea: Top management has the highest level of motivation, middle management has an average level of motivation, and ordinary employees have a low level of motivation. What an outrageous idea! I have seen a lot of «ordinary» employees who were at the duty level of motivation, and top executives whose level of motivation wasn't any higher than the personal gain level. As I listened to this person speak, I thought of my parents, both highly qualified workers. When they were young, they often had friends over for dinner, and I, while still a little boy, listened with pleasure to what the adults were discussing at the table. During these dinners, the conversation inevitably turned from local and personal matters to industrial ones; my mother and father really liked and enjoyed their jobs. I don't know whether they had a duty level of motivation, but at the very least they had a personal conviction level.

If you ask the average person about his or her personal goals and what he or she wants to achieve in life, you will discover a terrible truth. Most of them do not have any personal goals. They lost their dreams and aspirations a long time ago. One has to admit that it is crazy that a person of approximately forty years of age would not be able to answer a question about what he wants to achieve in life. Incidentally, most of them will not want to talk to you at all. They will feel uncomfortable discussing the subject of their personal goals. Do you know why? Because deep in their hearts they know that this lack of personal goals makes their life pointless. When you ask them questions about their personal goals, they briefly consider the subject and see a frightening abyss. That is why they will talk to you about anything trivial—sports, politics, or the weather, but not about their personal goals. It is too scary and painful to do so.

How have people sunk to this state? I believe it is due to rejection and disappointment. This process begins in childhood. A child says he wants to become a fireman and ride a big red truck, and his horrified parents heatedly tell him that he needs to become a lawyer like his mother or father. He wants a huge teddy bear, but he is emphatically told that he cannot have one due to some strange reason known only to them. If you look at a child's life, you will see it is far from easy. He is completely dependent on the will of those around him. He cannot have anything without the approval and assistance of adults. There is almost nothing he can do other than what is suggested by his parents. In many families and schools, a child learns that he cannot achieve anything and that there is something wrong with his goals. Have you ever tried very hard to get something, only to find every door slammed in your face? What emotions did you experience in that moment? If you're like most people, you felt mental anguish and disappointment. If, in a person's life, there are too many moments when his aspirations caused him mental anguish, sooner or later he will try to avoid this pain by refusing to think about his personal goals.

In 1993, I worked for the Time Manager International Company, which provided training on improving personal effectiveness. One of the training components was setting up personal goals for the next twenty years and beyond. When I first began to think about my particular goals, I felt as if I had a concrete slab on my shoulders. Back then, I thought it was normal to feel this way when pondering goals. Nonetheless, I continued planning and setting goals for a few years ahead, and eventually it became easier and easier for me. It is a bit like a fear of heights. One day when I was a kid, my friends and I decided to climb up a fire tower. When we reached the top, I was so afraid that I could not even stand up. I was on all fours, breathless with fear. At that moment, I did not know that going back down was going to be even worse! But after climbing this tower a few more times, I started feeling more confident. Eventually, I could stand and begin to notice the beautiful surroundings and enjoy the vast space around me. It is the same with goals. When you first start to plan your own life, the initial steps don't bring you any enjoyment. They are difficult to make, but you'll find that the longer you work at it, the more enjoyment it brings.

When you deal with people, you should understand that the majority of them are like scared children and cannot look at their future. If you force them to look, it is so unbearable to some that they would prefer to attack you and your ideas, anything not to think about the future. This should not stop you, of course. You should just draw their attention to the company's goals. Continue to do it, and sooner or later they will begin to accept the company's goals, although they may be resistant in the very beginning.

In essence, a person gets to the duty level of motivation in working for a company only when he shares the main goals of that company. It is simple and complex at the same time. It is simple because all you need to do is promote these goals to every employee of the company. It is complex because it takes time and there are obstacles that you will need to overcome.

Another false idea with regard to goals is that in order to have a high level of motivation, people first need to satisfy their basic needs. For example, in order for people to have a desire to do any kind of creative work, they first need to be well fed, feel safe, et cetera. This is complete nonsense. Look at people who are truly passionate about what they do. They very often do not care at all about food and living conditions. Just think of examples of people who have given up their health and their lives in order to achieve their goals. Take business owners, many of whom started their businesses during very uncertain times. They risked a great deal, spent all of their time at work, invested all of their money, and even borrowed money to invest, putting themselves and their families at risk. Only an individual who has never taken on any significant goals would say that in order to be inspired to achieve them, he has to have his basic needs satisfied first. Never swallow this bait. The employees of your company can accept and support the company's goals no matter what their salary is or what level of material well-being the company provides at the time.

The adoption of these false ideas about creating motivation leads to the illusion that there exists a vicious cycle with regard to motivation. Someone might say, «In order for personnel to have a high level of motivation, it is important to pay them well. In order to be able to pay them well, you need high revenues. It is only possible to have high revenues when people work with a high level of dedication, but a high level of motivation is required to work with a high level of dedication.»

This is a vicious cycle, but is only an illusion, as it is not necessary to have high revenues to increase your employees' level of motivation. You simply need to inspire them with lofty goals. I am not claiming, however, that money does not have any influence on motivation.

The level of a person's motivation depends on where that person's attention is directed. You know very well that when your attention is focused on something you find very interesting, you do not even see or hear what is happening around you. When you are fascinated by an interesting book, movie, or your favorite hobby, even if cannons fired around, you would pay no attention to them. Time stops and other things no longer exist for you. When a person is really engrossed in something, she could even get injured and not even notice. If a person's attention is focused on shared goals, she will be fascinated and feel a sense of duty. If the goals are not realistic to her, she cannot concentrate on them. Instead, she will be focused on her own principles, and her level of motivation will be that of personal conviction. If even her own principles are not real to her but only the benefits she needs are, she will operate on a personal gain level of motivation. The better you can focus a person's attention on the company's goals, the higher the level of motivation will be.

Do not forget that life does not consist of work alone. People move along the streets and see advertisements that urge them to buy things, reminding them of the necessity of making money. They return home and their family members also remind them of the necessity of making money. They meet with friends, who also tell them about the necessity of money. So while you are focusing people's attention on the company's goals, there are a lot of other things in their lives that focus their attention on money and personal gain. That is why the worse the compensation situation is, the more difficult it is for a leader to perform his duty to focus an employee's attention on the company's goals. The more problems at home a person has, the more frequently you have to remind him of these goals. It can also be noted that while money issues and problems at home can really lower a person's motivation, a high salary and good benefits on their own will never be able to increase it. That is why you cannot simply discuss goals one time, inspire your employees, and then relax. The attention you have focused on the company's goals will quickly be refocused on money and benefits if you do not constantly redirect it back to the chosen goals of the organization.

Chapter 7

Goal Promotion

The easiest way to instill a new idea in the mind of another person is to tell him about it. When you're just starting your business, gather together all of your friends, relatives, and those who did not manage to escape when they saw that crazy gleam in your eyes, and tell them about your genius idea. The kinds of responses you get to your idea will depend on the types of people you have surrounded yourself with in life. Surround yourself with skeptics, and they will trample on even the most brilliant idea. The future is probably the most fragile thing that people have to consider, and it is the easiest target for destructive criticism. Make negative comment about a concrete building and it will not even waver. But a dream envisioned by an individual can be destroyed irrevocably. That is why over the years we become more cautious, like army sappers in a minefield, in our endeavors to share our ideas with others. In most cases, others criticize your dreams simply because someone has trampled on theirs. Find a man who does not believe in the possibility of great achievements, and you will see a miserable man. That is probably why Napoléon had only fortunate people as his generals; he surrounded himself with men who in that environment could help him implement his grandiose plans.

When I was planning to start my first manufacturing business for the production of medals and souvenirs, my business partners had many reasons why my idea was not feasible. When I proposed that they cooperate in the implementation of my idea, an expert with a lot of experience asked me with undisguised skepticism, «Young man, what do you know about medals?» He was outraged at the idea that someone could dream about the field where he had worked all of his life, and where he had already buried so many of his own dreams. In 1954, when Ray Kroc burned with the idea to create McDonald's, he was over fifty years old, and it was his eighth attempt at creating the company of his dreams. Even the McDonald brothers did not believe that he could create a prosperous franchise chain. In 1961, they demanded that Kroc buy their rights for the trademark, and they left the business before the company started making profits.

Don't be surprised if you hear no applause when you first tell the managers and employees of your company about its main goal. If during a routine meeting or conference, you depart from the usual topics and suddenly say, «And now I want to tell you what the main goal of our company is» the most likely outcome will be something like the following. Some very loyal employees will look at you with astonishment and admiration, but most will be asking themselves, *Why is he telling us that?* Some might be asking themselves, *But the goal of a business is to make money, isn't it?* The way they react to your announcement will be merely a reflection of their own motivation. Those who operate on duty level of motivation will get confirmation of their ideas and will be inspired. Those who are on the personal conviction level will think that talking about goals is just part of your job and will treat this with understanding, even if they have not yet accepted the goal. Finally, those who operate on the personal gain and money levels of motivation will think that you have some kind of selfish or ulterior motive, that perhaps you just want to get some benefit for yourself. People always interpret what you tell them about goals through the prism of their own personal level of motivation. Incidentally, this is often the reason some unwise wives nag their husbands (or vice versa) for focusing enough on their jobs. The level of motivation of such spouses with respect to their partners' professional activities is personal gain. If they were really keen on inspiring their partners to heroic deeds (which corresponds with, at least, the personal conviction level of motivation with respect to their relationship with their partners), their lives would become significantly more harmonious.

In 2003, my partner at Geroldmaster (an outstanding designer and creator of numerous state and departmental medals in Ukraine) and I formulated the main goal and purpose of the company. I will never forget the reaction of our employees when we introduced it to them. During a general meeting, I announced that the goal of the company was to shape the Ukrainian people's self-identity as a nation with rich cultural and historical traditions. It was like a moment of silence in memory of fallen heroes. Still, I fully intended to convey this idea to our employees. During every subsequent meeting, I tried to mention this goal and give examples showing how we were gradually achieving it. I told them that a number of medals that were designed and manufactured by our company had made it into the Museum of Ukrainian History, and about how entire displays in this museum were filled with our products, as well as information about the people who had received these medals. Over time, I noticed that this goal was becoming more and more real to our employees. Climbing up the scale of motivation, they began asking whether we faced any obstacles and how we could overcome them. When they began asking such questions, I realized that their attention had become partially focused on the company's goal, and that they had started to gradually recognize and understand it. Of course, this certainly did not happen over the course of the first or second meeting. It took a few months before the goal became more or less real to them. If you want to change people's outlook, you must arm yourself with time and patience. You may ask, Why do I, the company's owner, need to have patience and constantly bring these ideas to my employees? Why do I have to settle all of these disagreements? There is only one reason for it: You did not do it from the beginning, and it is neither easy nor fun to correct mistakes. That is why you will need time and patience.

When a company is growing, its managers should begin to promote the company's main goal as part of their job. This raises a new problem. If the managers operate on a personal gain level of motivation, they will never be able to convey the company's goal to their staff. They will distort it, presenting it through a prism of their own motives. Instead of focusing attention on the benefits that the company brings to society, they will talk about the benefits that the company gains. It is therefore important that during the company's growth phase you, as the formulator of the goals, do not sever the line of communication with employees and that you continue to remind them of the main goal during staff meetings and in documents stating company policies. The larger your company becomes, the more time you will need to devote to this task, because ideology is the most powerful tool in the management of large groups. Before you delegate the job of presenting your company's goal to anyone else, make sure that person is at the duty level of motivation. People quickly sense insincerity, and thus such promotion of the goal by someone at less than the duty level of motivation would undermine its credibility.

The worst harm you can inflict on a group is to make its goals lose value. The collapse of the strongest groups in the history of mankind began with the destruction of their goals. Why did the Roman Empire decline and fall? Its leaders and its people lost sight of Rome's civilizing purpose and goals. In the transition from the Roman Republic to the domination of imperial rulers, the stern virtues of citizens were undermined by the increasingly servile mind-set and self-indulgence of the ruled. The Romans, as a group, clearly abandoned the core purposes, vision, and discipline that had enabled Rome, at its peak, to spread its domains from Britain to the Euphrates, from the Rhine to Egypt and Asia Minor.

Anyone who criticizes the main goal of a group causes it significant harm. If a person does not agree with the goals of a company, he does not necessarily need to work there. However, while he does work there and is a part of that group, it is in his best interest that the group remains strong. This is a simple precept, but people who lack knowledge in management do not even realize that they are destroying their own future by not abiding by this rule of thumb. Fortunately, business is one of those fields where no one demands a democracy and an owner is free to define goals independently without considering the opinions of his employees. Therefore, simply forming and promoting goals is not enough. Your task is also to discourage criticism of these goals. If you want to have a strong group, there should be no room for people who openly, or secretly, denounce the goals of the group.

In his article about the roles of goal suppliers and managers, L. Ron Hubbard wrote:

Goals for companies or governments are usually a dream, dreamed first by one man, then embraced by a few and finally held up as the guidon of the many.

Part of a goal is its glamour and part of any dream is the man who dreamed it[5].

The person who creates the goal is a part of the goal. While it is not easy to criticize a goal that is targeted to benefit people, it is much easier to criticize the person who created it. In order for your goals and your group to be strong, it is important to remember that you need: to discourage criticism derided at you by others.

Remember that any person who criticizes the supplier of goals personally harms the whole group, no matter what his motives for doing so may be. There cannot be any «healthy criticism» directed at the one who has established the goals, because he no longer represents himself alone. Instead, he becomes a sort of symbol of the goals, and his image as the leader and goal setter is no longer a personal matter. It is a standard for the group. It should also be added that positivity should also be a part of this image. This means that various kinds of sanctions, including dismissals of even the most negligent of employees, should not be carried out by or on behalf of the individual who provides the goals for the organization.

---

[5] L. Ron Hubbard, «An Essay on Management», in The Management Series, vol.1 (Los Angeles: Bridge Publications, 2001), 4–5.

The dreamer of dreams and the user of flogs on lazy backs cannot be encompassed in the same man, for the dream to be effective, must be revered, and the judge and the taskmaster can only be respected[6].

You have managers to administer discipline. Do not allow them to shift disciplinary responsibilities onto the goal supplier. Your job is to inspire the whole group to victory.

Intuition should tell you that a mundane work routine and the establishment of inspiring goals do not mix well. It is difficult to look into the future when on a daily basis you have to solve a number of minor, uninspiring problems and promptly address issues that arise. That is why a distinction between business owners' functions and managers' functions is a correct state of affairs. An owner, as the goal supplier, should oversee all of the activities of the company in general, establish its strategic direction, and assess its overall condition. The business owner is on the front line and extracts maximum results out from the company.

---

[6] L. Ron Hubbard, «An Essay on Management», in The Management Series, vol.1 (Los Angeles: Bridge Publications, 2001), 5.

Chapter 8

....

Establishing the Future

For several years, my colleagues and I organized tours to Dubai for business owners who had completed the Business Owners Program. We arranged excursions to local businesses and sightseeing attractions, and held workshops on strategic business development. During a final event, such as a gala dinner, we handed out diplomas that certified the recipients had mastered the implementation of management tools. Dubai was chosen for a reason. Although it is not a symbol of entrepreneurship, this country is an inspiring example of the practical application of the most important management tools.

Forty years ago, Dubai was still a backward country and its population suffered from a lack of food and water. People lived in huts with dirt floors and dreamed of the day when they would have enough water. Among Dubai's native people who are over fifty years old, you will meet almost no one who was born in the summer. The reason is very simple: Children who were born in summer usually died from the heat or from malnourishment in infancy. One Arab I know told me that during Soviet times he was a member of a group of Arabic boys who went to Moscow to study at the Moscow State University. A faucet with running water seemed like an unbelievable miracle to them. They got together in one of their rooms and cried because they realized how terrible the living conditions of their people were. They were shocked by the standard of living in Moscow, with its stone buildings and abundance of water and food.

That was over four decades ago. Nowadays, our fellow Russians visit Dubai and admire its beautiful buildings, perfect roads, and the highest standards of service. The Dubai subway is one of the most modern in the world. Nowhere in the world have I seen a better balance of luxury and comfort in hotels. Affordable prices as well as high-quality food and service make a stay in Dubai especially enjoyable. Architects and designers from all over the world have seen their boldest ideas transformed into reality in Dubai. That is why the tallest building in the world, the first skyscraper with rotating floors, the largest malls, and an artificial ski resort constructed inside the Mall of the Emirates are all in Dubai. The construction of the first solar power station in the world with 1GW[7] capacity, which will significantly lower the cost of producing electricity and reduce the amount carbon dioxide emissions released into the atmosphere, is scheduled to get under way in Dubai's desert in 2015.

One could certainly say that the reason for this miracle is oil. However, let us compare, for example, the amount of oil produced per capita in Dubai with the amount of oil produced in Russia. Dubai produces about 80,000 barrels[8] of oil per day, while Russia produces about 10,270,000 barrels per day. Dubai produces sixteen barrels of oil per capita each year, while Russia produces twenty-six barrels of oil per capita each year. It should also be noted that in contrast to Russia, Dubai has almost no natural resources other than oil. Obviously, the key to the success of the country is not its natural resources. There is something more important.

In 1969, when oil production started in Dubai, it was apparent that its oil reserves were rather limited, but a brilliant strategy to rationally utilize this resource allowed the emir of Dubai to turn a backward country into a symbol of the world's highest standards. How was this accomplished? There are a few important things that have contributed to this success.

First, Dubai has a monarchical form of government, where power is inherited, but it does not necessarily pass from father to son. The monarch appoints a crown prince, who becomes the emir after the monarch's death. In this way, the monarch ensures there is enough time for the heir to the throne to adopt his ideology, strategy, and governance methods. There is no apparent power struggle. The source of authority is stable, and there is an opportunity to realize long-term plans without fear that authority will pass to someone with different views on development. Look at what happened to Apple's stock price after Steve Jobs passed away. It went down because nobody believed that under Tim Cook's leadership the company's successful strategy would remain unchanged.

Second, the emir of Dubai worked skillfully to ensure that Dubai's domestic strategy was recognized and supported throughout the world. In essence, he made the entire world recognize Dubai as a prosperous and growing country. During the period from 1971 to 1979, Dubai's largest trading port was built. In 1984, a law was passed for the benefit of trading companies that improved opportunities

---

[7] One gigawatt (GW) is equal to one billion watts. This is enough energy to power ten million 100-Watt light bulbs.

[8] One barrel of oil is equivalent to approximately forty-two U.S. gallons.

for international trade through Dubai's ports. In 1985, a law on free economic zones[9] was passed. What is interesting is that to this day, Dubai remains a virtually tax-free country. The government utilizes revenues from natural resources, government enterprises, and various licenses. All of this creates a basis for future growth, but on its own this would not lead to rapid growth. The following quote clearly explains what happened next.

Money could be called an attention unit of society. It flows through the society and is sort of mocked-up[10]; they're really attention units[11] that flow through the society. If you don't believe that, you want to make a lot of money, just attract a lot of attention. Of course, if you attract the attention on the «have-not» basis, everybody will take the money the other way, so that's all right[12].

In 1994, the Jumeirah International Group, owned by the ruler of Dubai, built a luxurious five-star deluxe hotel, the Burj Al Arab. The hotel was situated on an artificial island approximately three hundred yards from shore. Since this hotel opened, it has remained a symbol of Dubai and has attracted the attention of the world. Everyone has seen pictures of this hotel in travel agencies' promotional materials. The construction and maintenance costs were such that by rough estimate, it is not profitable. At the same time, it is one of the most luxurious hotels in the world.

In 2001, another company, Nakheel, also owned by the ruler of Dubai, embarked on the grandiose project of constructing an artificial island in the Persian Gulf called Palma Jumeirah. From the time the construction began until 2006, when the first building was built, this project attracted enormous attention. It has been called the «Eighth Wonder of the World.» As a result of this project, the coastline of Dubai has doubled in length. Now, twenty of the most popular and luxurious hotels are located on this island.

In 2004, the largest shopping mall in the world, Dubai Mall, was built. In 2009, the tallest building in the world, Burj Khalifa (2,717

---

[9] Free economic zones are areas where little or no taxation is made upon companies in order to encourage business growth and improve the economy.

[10] A mock-up is an image that is consciously created in the mind. This term is used to distinguish a consciously created image from images that arise in the mind subconsciously. If you imagine a smooth red rubber ball, you create a mock-up in your mind to look at.

[11] Units of attention are the rays of energy, that are sent by people toward something in order to gain perception. People are able to physically feel the attention. Just remember a situation when all of a sudden, felt that someone was looking at you, and then turned around and saw that it was true.

[12] L. Ron Hubbard, Lecture #73, in The Philadelphia Doctorate Course Lectures, vol.4 (Los Angeles: Golden Era Productions 2007), 400.

feet), was constructed. Interestingly, these and many other iconic objects were built by the Arab world's largest real estate development corporation, Emaar Properties, 32 percent of which is owned by the ruler of Dubai.

Consistently, year after year, the government ensured that interest in Dubai as a technologically advanced country increased. As soon as attention focused on one project lessened, a new project was started. This has resulted in Dubai's becoming one of the most investment-attractive countries in the world. Worldwide people have invested in real estate in the Persian Gulf area. Even among some of my friends, there are a few who have got purchased real estate in Dubai. What an excellent embodiment of the idea of using the principle of «pro-survival» to attract attention. Why is the idea of using the principle of pro-survival advantageous? Well, a company attracts contra-survival attention when it is unable to pay its debts or has other problems.

I do not mention all of this to glorify the Dubai emirs or to advertise real estate. Personally, I am very skeptical about investing a business' revenue in overseas real estate. There is some kind of injustice toward one's own business when doing this. It would be like taking positive energy away from successful operations and transferring it to an area over which you have no control, or like robbing a successful entrepreneur of his or her money and giving it to others who have yet to prove that they are capable of doing anything worthwhile. I believe the best place for any investment of money earned by a business is back into the business itself. If any other enterprise seems more attractive to you for investment, then you clearly have motivation issues to address.

When you form the goals of your business, you must face the fact that while your goals are only on paper and not yet implemented, they are not real to other people. The more you create tangible evidence that attracts people's attention, the more real the goals become. Regardless of what business you are in or how large your business is, you can invest a portion of your energy and capital into the creation of material symbols that make your dreams more real.

When you open a new office, you can make a major event out of it, thereby attracting a number of potential customers' and partners' pro-survival attention. At the beginning of this year, we opened a new office in the far eastern area of Russia (just across the Sea of Japan.) It was a small, nicely renovated office (about 1,615 square feet). We invited the local press, government officials, and public figures. We announced that the international company Visotsky Consulting, Inc., was opening an office to assist local businesses with the implementation of management tools. We also gave them an idea of how the business results of our clients had changed after they consulted with us, which generated interest in our operations. The event was featured on all the news channels and I gave several interviews to the local press.

When Apple releases a new product, a grand event is carefully planned in advance to fuel interest in the product. Meanwhile the product's features are shrouded in secrecy. In doing this, Apple turns each new release into an event that attracts an enormous amount of public attention. As soon as the product is announced, the company begins working to generate public interest in the next product.

In 2001, when Steve Jobs was going to open Apple stores, he was told that his idea of opening a specialized, single-brand computer store in a mall was crazy. Computers were not considered boutique items, and it was not customary to sell them in the same place where fashionable clothes were sold. Despite objections from industry specialists, which Jobs never really considered anyway, he created a new style of computer store. The first two stores were in Glendale, California, and McLean, Virginia. During their two-day grand opening, they received a combined total of over 7,700 visitors and sold $599,000 in merchandise. To date, the Apple stores are retailing leaders in terms of sales per square foot. Best Buy, which at the time was one of the leading sellers of computers and electronic devices, earned about $850 per square foot per year. Apple achieved a record of $6,050 per square foot per year. Well-designed and done in a uniform style mandated by Jobs, a style set for every Apple store throughout the world, Apple stores attracted a huge amount of attention for the company's products, and the shops themselves became the model of the new format for computer sales.

While working with entrepreneurs, I frequently encounter the opinion that image-building campaigns are just a waste of money. But if money is lost in such an endeavor, this is the result of incompetence. A company's public image is incredibly important. The more attractive and interesting a company looks, the greater the customers' desire to part with their money for its products or services, and the more motivation for its employees to work hard for its success. One of our clients, a café owner serving Iranian ethnic cuisine, began hosting unusual events his premise. On Sunday mornings when the café was not busy, he set up workshops on baking meat pies. Experienced chefs shared their secrets with attendees and taught people how to bake these pies. When journalists heard about the workshops, a story about them made it onto a local television news channel. In addition, workshop attendees shared the pleasure of their experience with friends and family, which attracted even more public attention. The café's revenues went up and the number of home-delivery sales increased.

As a result of the 2007 economic crisis, which reached the Ukrainian print industry by the fall of 2008 and peaked in 2010, the print industry found itself in a fine pickle. Magazine circulation at the largest publishers fell. The largest advertisers cut their advertising budgets, and the fight for new orders became a fight for anyone company's life. As often happens during such times, severe price dumping began in the industry. However, the Ukrainian printing company Triada-Print, instead of following the example of the majority of companies and freezing spending on improvements to its production area, acquired an ultramodern Japanese-manufactured printing press. This machine provided an advantage in the production costs of medium-size runs. In 2011, the equipment was fully installed and brought into operation. Naturally, there had to be a significant number orders for the press run to be cost-effective, but how could this be done in an industry where most of the equipment was idle and companies fiercely competed for orders, slashing prices to acquire customers? In order to draw attention to the benefits of its new machine, Triada-Print held a megapresentation of the new production line. They invited the world's most renowned guru from the magazine industry and held a huge party for publishers, where all the most popular magazine-publishing figures and the press were present. The occasion consisted of two main events. The first was a presentation by the magazine guru, and the second was the presentation of the new printing machine. Of course, this event was featured in all of the magazines and other print media. And do you know what is most interesting? In 2012, using the new equipment, this company printed almost all of the glossy magazines in circulation in Ukraine, a very desirable piece of the pie for a company in the print industry. However, if you think that the owners of Triada-Print had bags of money to invest in high-end equipment and promotion, you are mistaken. The company had experienced the effects of the economic crisis just as their competitors had. However, the Triada-Print owners had a rational and long-term vision, and they put all their efforts into its implementation. I know for certain that doing this was not easy.

The more one's employees are inspired by significant company achievements, the more real the company's goals become. The more attention that employees direct toward those goals, the sooner they are accomplished. What is a prosperous company? It is a company that everyone agrees is prosperous. This sounds like magic, but when it comes to people management, it really is true. If you are able to convince people that your company makes the best product, your product will actually become the best. It's all about perception. Perhaps your competitors can prove that their product is technically more convenient to use, faster, or cheaper. But who cares about all of that if customers prefer your product? People buy what they consider is best suited to their needs, not what is the best on the market.

In creating the future of the company, you are, in fact, materializing ideas, and there is a secret that helps get people to agree with your ideas more readily. It is a fact that the material universe functions according to certain laws. One of the fundamental laws is that regarding the conservation of energy. Since matter is actually a form of concentrated, or stored, energy, it is subject to this law. Matter can easily be converted into energy simply by burning fuel, but the inverse is more difficult to perform, which is why it is not as popular. In any case, in the material universe, this law applies to energy and to matter. It is impossible to build a house without bricks, it is impossible to produce bricks without clay, and so on. Everything that exists in the material universe is created from a transformation of one object into another. But this occurs only in the material universe.

The human mind works differently. There was a time when you were the same as everyone around you. You went to the same school with other kids and then to a similar type of university. Then, perhaps, you worked somewhere. At some point, you decided to become an entrepreneur, and did so. You could say that your education and your experience predetermined your future, but it would not be true. Many other people received a similar education and had similar experiences, but they did not become entrepreneurs. At school, my friends and I made fashionable shirts of cheap fabric, colored them with a blue dye so that they looked like denim, imitating the appearance and texture of famous brands, by using colored silicone sealant for bathrooms. We also copied audiotapes of Western singers, spending nights making these copies on reel-to-reel tape recorders, then sold them to classmates, making enough money for beer and entertainment. (Back in those days, the Soviet Union was not particularly concerned with copyright protection!) It was my first entrepreneurial experience. I will admit that I wasn't the one who got everyone going in all of these enterprises, but interestingly, I was the only one who became a business owner. The others are all now employed in companies. Why is that?

It is not a matter of the experience or knowledge you have gained. Most of us have never actually studied entrepreneurship. It is all a matter of the decisions one makes. I had a childhood friend, a very kind and peace-loving person, who was often bullied. One day, he made a decision to become stronger so that no one could hurt him anymore. After a while, he became the leader of a local gang. A person can make decisions and change them in accordance with the role he plays in life. It doesn't even require much time; in fact, it can happen instantly. Material conditions in this case are irrelevant (unless, of course, your decision has something to do with your body, because that is tangible, which is why you should not decide that you are some superhero and have the ability to jump from skyscrapers).

This ability to change as the need arises is why at any time you can set whatever future for your company you desire, and it will be completely reasonable. As the goal supplier, only your own desire matters and there is no reason to realize any other version of the future. As an example, imagine that for the past ten years you have been the owner of a café, and for the last five years your business has stayed at the same level. In other words, it has not grow or improved. What prevents you from one day (and, why not today?) making the decision to start a successful international café chain and beginning to promote this idea to your employees? Do you know what would most likely happen? They would not believe you. Most people are accustomed to, and very agreeable with, the physical laws of the material universe. They would look at their experiences over the past few years and tell you that your goal is impossible and that it could not happen, simply because it had never happened before. Would they be right? Of course not. The past has almost nothing to do with our future. A majority of international chain founders did something for the first and the last time in their lifetimes. Before starting McDonald's, Ray Kroc had never owned a café or restaurant. Steve Jobs had never been a talented engineer or a programmer. The parents of Standard Oil's[13] founder, John D. Rockefeller, were simple workers.

The secret if you want people to quickly accept your ideas about the future is to show them real examples that convince them that the past foreshadows the future. This is the basis of an overused but still beautifully effective method that has been employed for thousands of years when someone has needed to convince people of the infallibility of some idea. Notice how the followers of different philosophies and ideas follow carefully the tales of leaders as children. One of many striking examples of this is the biography by Walter Isaacson, Steve Jobs, which includes stories about Jobs's life. Why is this of such interest to people? Because they want to find the material evidence of his success. For the same reason, many corporations publish books and create museums that show different aspects of the life of the founder

---

[13] Standard Oil, an American corporation that, as noted previously, produced, transported, and refined oil. It was established by the merger of several American companies. The company was prosecuted under antitrust laws and broken up into thirty-four smaller, independent companies, among which were companies like Exxon, Sohio, Amoco, Mobil Gas, Chevron, and Marathon Oil Corporation.

of the company and the company's history. Naturally, these books and museums tend to show exactly those events that contain material evidence of past successes that thereby demonstrate achievable future goals. For example, the story of Steve Jobs's calligraphy classes testifies to the fad that Apple's products are best suited for working with fonts and use in publishing. Recently, I was at the clinic of a famous doctor in New Jersey. In his office hung framed newspaper articles in which something good was written about him. When you go into the room and see that for decades he has had a good track record, it creates confidence that his future will be even more successful. This does not mean that you need to make up anything, as throughout the lifetime of your company there will have been lots of victories to which you can direct your employees' attention.

If you simply describe the history of your company as a series of achievements, and present these achievements as stepping-stones to the goals you are promoting, then in no time you will make these goals seem more achievable to everyone. Have you ever heard artists or writers talk about how their works were created? These are stories about long meditations and anguish, about creative endeavor and painstaking work. This is just a necessary part of the game to make it easier for people to understand the tremendous value of the artwork. Could a painting be considered a work of genius if it were done in one session, in a single day? No, it would only be considered a work of genius if the person who created it spent decades of hard work and incredible creative efforts in order to achieve such a level of mastery. The history of your company and your personal history as a goal provider should also look like a clear path of events that predetermined your success.

Uninformed people will tell you that the history of your company and your own achievements are too positive. They will tell you that there were mistakes, too, and that you, as the owner, are no saint. For these people, the truth is only that which can be touched. The real truth, however, lies whatever future you create. When Ray Kroc sold the first McDonald's franchise, he embellished income statements to make them look more attractive to people who invested their money and efforts into the business. As a result, he created the largest restaurant chain in the world, and his franchisees were grateful to him. Kroc conducted inspirational seminars on his business in which he presented examples of his existing restaurants' successes. What did all of these examples have to do with the future franchisee rookies? Nothing, but it made the goals more real, and if the rookie franchisee believed the goals were achievable, then he or she would achieve them in real life.

So while creating an amazing future for your company, forget about the vulgar ideas of modesty and realism, which are usually peddled by people who have never created anything remarkable in their entire lives. Creating the future begins with the agreement of others on this future, and it makes sense to work on building this agreement.

Chapter 9

....

The Product and the Brand

These days, the roles of advertising and sales are talked about a great deal. The success of a company is considered to be fully dependent on how well it can sell its products. But let's be honest about this. How many shoe stores are there in your city where you can find shoes to your liking? How many restaurants are there that you would unreservedly recommend to your friends? How many construction companies would you gladly endorse to your acquaintances when they need to build a house or renovate a building? Look around— in the United States or in any other country in the world. You will find that just about anywhere you can create a business that will have satisfied customers. It requires only that someone clearly define what product the company will produce.

There are no universal products. Every product is tailored for a particular type of customer. Attempting to please everyone generates very strange products. Naturally, the more narrow and precise the product positioning, the more perfect it will be upon creation. When Ray Kroc first started selling McDonald's franchises, there were franchisees who tried to arrange to have waiters and tables covered with tablecloths. They tried to distort the product of the restaurant in order to please a wide range of customers, including those who preferred a traditional dining atmosphere. If Ray Kroc, with the assistance of his finance director, Harry Sonneborn, had not found a way to keep franchisees under control[14], the franchisees' creativity, combined with liberal legislation, would have led to an army of small competitors instead of one famous restaurant.

Behind every great product there is a person who defines its basic standards. After ten years, during which he built Pixar, Steve Jobs returned to Apple. During his absence, the company produced a whole range of various products: an entire line of desktop and laptop computers, laser printers and scanners, Newton PDAs, computer

---

[14] The company began to lease land on a long-term basis to build restaurants at its own expense and then rent it to franchisees. This provided the opportunity to exert influence upon unscrupulous franchisees, who infringed on standards established by the corporation.

monitors, and more. By the time Jobs returned, the company had experienced cumulative annual losses of $1.2 billion. Upon obtaining the necessary authority, Jobs canceled 75 percent of the product line. A year after his return to the company, annual revenues exceeded $300 million. Creative managers and technical experts, whose desire was to satisfy the demands of a wide range of customers, almost put the company out of business. Essentially, Jobs just returned the company's product line to the vision that he, as the founder, considered to be correct. Over the next ten years, the products created under his direction made the company a world leader.

In a list of the top ten most successful franchising companies, there is one cleaning company — Servpro Industries — that specializes in repairing fire and flood damage. In 1969, they started franchising, and now the company has over sixteen hundred franchisees. I am sure that the idea of providing a wider range of services repeatedly came to the minds of the employees, and that a great number of customers recommended expanding the range of services offered by the company. But would this company be as successful if it had tried to expand the range of services it provided?

When I arrived in New York for the first time, one of the very first things I observed was the deliberate specialization of American companies. Even restaurant menus differed from Ukrainian ones. In a pretty nice seafood restaurant, Oceana, located near Times Square, the whole menu fit on one page. It included four types of salads, four types of soups, four main courses, a few side dishes, and that was it! But each of these dishes was a masterpiece of culinary art, executed with invariable skill. This was very much in contrast to Ukrainian restaurants, where the salad options alone spread across four pages and the main courses take up another three. I doubt that all of the dishes in such a restaurant are equally good, which is why an experienced food lover elicits the help of a waiter to find out which dishes are the best.

Recently, a restaurateur told me a story of how one of his acquaintances went to a nice restaurant specializing in Georgian cuisine, and left wondering why it was considered anything special. When this restaurateur was asked which dishes she had ordered, her reply was that she had ordered the Caesar salad and borsht. When asked why she had ordered those dishes in a Georgian restaurant, she said that she wanted to evaluate the skills of the kitchen by comparing its dishes with those of other restaurants, and in order to do so, she had ordered food that could be found in nearly any restaurant.

The point here is not her rather odd point of view. The question is why was a Georgian restaurant offering its customers these dishes at all? It is obvious that a person who orders Caesar salad and borsht at this restaurant will never become a fan, will not remember the experience positively, and will not be satisfied. Does it make sense to include these types of dishes on the menu at all, simply to please everyone? If they had not been on the menu, the waiter would have recommended something else to her, something that was a specialty of Georgian cuisine or a specialty of the chef, and she would have left pleased and told her friends about it. Borsht is borsht in any restaurant.

If you have never been to a Broadway musical, you should definitely go. For some reason, I had a preconceived bias against Broadway — probably something imposed by Soviet propaganda. When I saw *The Lion King* at the Minskoff Theatre in Times Square, I was amazed at the quality of the actors, the incredible scenery, and the wonderful music. Interestingly, in 2014 *The Lion King* overtook *Phantom of the Opera* as the stage musical with the most successful box-office income of any work in any media in entertainment history. Why change anything if it is a successful product that the public likes? The longer the public retains its interest in it, the more the production can be improved. *The Phantom of the Opera* continues to sell out at the nearby Majestic Theatre. It was first performed in 1988 and has since been staged for the public more than ten thousand times. Do you think it has become better or worse? There is even a rating of Broadway musicals based on a very simple assessment principle: how long the musical is able to draw a full house. As you know, customers vote for products with their dollars.

It is not possible to create a world-class product by trying to provide everything for everyone. In order to provide an outstanding product, it is necessary to develop good technological and organizational processes. How could you possibly develop good business processes if you are producing hundreds of different products, each with its own unique characteristics? It's no wonder that specialized companies win in the small to medium-size business markets. Of course, there are also corporations like Samsung, which produces a wide range of products — from home electronics to computers to cars. But can you name a product in which it is the leader? Except for low-budget TVs, nothing else comes to my mind. Even this giant has a hard time because it has to compete in a number of directions. In the tablet-manufacturing market, it competes with Apple. In the car-manufacturing market, it competes with Hyundai. In computer manufacturing, it competes with Toshiba and Acer. Perhaps a company of this magnitude can afford to do this, but a small company cannot.

Of course, it is important to follow the wishes of customers, but what do we mean by customers? When you start a company, you create it for a particular type of customer — for example, a restaurant for those who have only fifteen minutes to eat. Interestingly, the majority of fast-food restaurants won over the U.S. market first, then spread throughout the world. One reason for this is that U.S. federal law does not require employers to provide their employees with a lunch break (though some states laws require employers to provide one), so employees usually have very little time to eat lunch. When you realize this, it becomes clear as to why the area near Wall Street is full of quick, cheap Chinese eateries. Many people have a bite to eat at these places during their lunch hour, even though they earn millions. This has formed a particular kind of customer and a unique food culture.

If you start a manufacturing company, you also target a particular type of customer. If it is a mid-level private company, then it is going to have a particular service level, type of advertising, and distribution channels. If you manufacture products of the highest quality, then you will have a completely different service level, different advertising, and different distribution channels. One type of customer prioritizes price, while another prioritizes design, comfort, and craftsmanship.

In our consulting business, we offer our Business Owners Program consulting project only to business owners, even though we are often asked to admit company executives who want to implement the management tools we have developed. In the history of our company, there were only a few special cases when we agreed to accept such executives (money is money, after all). The results were as follows: One executive, after implementing management tools that led to a significant increase in revenues, became a co-owner of the company. Another implemented the management tools, then left the company in order to start his own business (thankfully, not a competing one). A third who implemented the management tools left and started a rival company. After this, a rule was established not to accept executives at our school any longer. Otherwise, we would be creating problems for the clients we worked with in exchange for the money they paid us. Why did we make these mistakes? It happened because no one was watching, or was watching very poorly, how our school met its intended purpose. We did not have precise rules and did not monitor whether they were being followed.

In 2003, I had to carry out a little «product-line revolution» at Geroldmaster. At that time, in addition to medals and metal souvenirs manufactured internally, the company offered customers a wide range of merchandise produced by other manufacturers. Usually, these were branded office products such as pens, clocks, and postcards. We simply accepted the order from the customer, designed the product, and outsourced it to another manufacturing facility. Such work provided about 20 percent of the revenues of the company, which was a pretty sizable slice of the pie. But there was also a dark side. If orders for outsourced products were large in proportion to in-house manufacturing orders, our own manufacturing facility sat idle, which caused us losses. Attempts to deal with this issue mathematically using calculations to decide whether this outsourced business caused more harm than good were unsuccessful.

When I carefully investigated how our sales department was working with customers, I found that sales volumes of internally manufactured products could not be any higher because it was often easier for a salesperson to sell pens with a company logo at a lower price tag than to sell more expensive corporate lapel pins (lapel pins with a company's corporate logo). Having analyzed this information, I realized that by providing customers with all of the choices available, we were destroying the future of our company. I had to make a very unpopular decision: We would stop offering products that we did not manufacture ourselves. The next day, the head of the sales department handed in his resignation. He left and started his own souvenir company, through which he found customers and placed their orders with other manufacturing facilities. I had to address the discontent of the salespeople who were paid on commission for third-party souvenir orders, as well as placate company executives who did not understand why I decided to give up such a significant part of our revenues.

At that time, the company was far from flourishing, but after a few months I began to see the result that was most important to me: The manufacturing facility workload had increased significantly. I believe, with good evidence to back it up, that the decision to stop selling third-party products (with the exception of the cases that contained our medals) was one of my best strategic decisions. It not only contributed to an increase in profits but also strengthened our company's brand and helped us stand out from competitors. If you look at it from the point of view of an owner's functions and responsibilities, I simply got the company to do exactly what it was initially created for.

An opportunity for additional earnings can very often mislead you on your way to success. It is important to resist such temptations and guide the company toward creating an outstanding product for the customer. When Ray Kroc established the principles of franchising McDonald's, he was tempted to make money on the delivery of food, equipment, and expendable packaging materials for franchisees.

However, he realized that this would be a deviation from his main product, as the main product of his company was a flawless process for franchisees. If he had gotten sidetracked by additional activities and prospective earnings, his company's efforts would have gone in a completely different direction, rather than toward creating its main product[15]. If Kroc had done this during the initial stage of his company's growth, his company most likely would have made higher profits initially, but it is unlikely that we would ever have heard about McDonald's as a world-renowned company.

There is another trap to be aware of in product development: not being interested in the opinions of customers about what they value the most in your product. Owners tend to get involved with solving problems that they can solve well. For example, when a printing company came to me for consulting services, I conducted interviews with its owners to find out what they considered their company's most important and valuable products. They told me it was their use of modern technologies for color accuracy and quality. However, when we surveyed a couple of dozen customers who regularly placed orders with the company, we found that the majority said that one of the qualities they considered most important was service, specifically the timeliness with which orders were executed. Though the company faced the discontent of customers because of by late orders on a daily basis and had to handle these, there was no one truly engaged in achieving timeliness with regard to order execution. Of course, everyone in the company was «working on it.» They held meetings and tried to come up with ways to deliver products on time to their customers. But the company was investing millions in improving the quality of production, and almost nothing in what was most important to the customer: timeliness.

After the survey had been conducted, it took me a pretty long time to convince the owners that it was not a joke, that timeliness really was a priority for their customers, and that customers believed (perhaps incorrectly) that the majority of printing companies produced about the same level of quality but that only a few produced on time. This does not mean that the owners, while producing the product, considered timeliness unimportant. It just means that in the long run, failure to deliver on time had become routine to them. But often such routines become the biggest roadblocks to making a company's products successful.

---

[15] Over time, McDonald's moved to centralized procurement of equipment and products. As a matter of policy, McDonald's does not make direct sales of food or materials to franchisees, instead organizing the supply of food and materials to restaurants through approved third-party suppliers.

For example, say that you go to a restaurant that cost hundreds of thousands of dollars to create. A talented chef was hired to work there, and a ton of money was spent on advertising the place. You enjoy a nice atmosphere and great food, but when you go to the rest room, a small but unfortunate thing, such as the absence of toilet tissue, can completely ruin your whole impression of the restaurant. The owner opened a wonderful restaurant, but he will probably never find out why his customers, who admire the food and decor, rarely return. As an expert, the owner may be focused on the kitchen, examining the delicacy of the cuisine, its flavors, and the appearance of the dishes. He may have no knowledge of the other components that make up the whole experience that his restaurant provides. Some time ago, when the restaurant was just starting, poorly maintained rest rooms were not a problem. But this time has passed. That is why it is important to survey customers on a regular bases regarding the quality of the services they have received. It is also important that the person who performs the service carefully reads the results of such surveys in order to understand whether the service needs to be improved and to identify the specific areas needing improvement. If a significant number of customers name the same deviation in quality, does it make any sense to put efforts and resources toward anything other than this deviation? Of course, the above does not mean that upon identifying such deviations you must rush to correct them, but it is necessary to draw conclusions about what was missing in the operating processes of the company that allowed such deviations to occur. For example, in the above-mentioned printing company, the most common reason deadlines were missed was that salespeople accepted rush orders. When the rush order was sent to the manufacturer, the whole production process was disturbed. The production plan would fall apart, and as a result the rush order caused a few other orders to miss their deadlines. In order to resolve this issue, the owner created a rule that rush orders would cost double the price. The number of urgent orders decreased by several fold, and failures to meet delivery dates virtually ceased. Of course, the company lost some urgent orders, which went to competitors. If you look at the situation closely, however, it becomes obvious that by accepting rush orders, which brought chaos to its operations, the company was not being fair to its best customers, who had placed their orders in advance. Usually, it is pretty easy to solve a problem if you know exactly what the problem is. In this case, it did not take millions of dollars to solve a problem that had existed for several years, and which was the most important from the customers point of view.

Sometimes marketing experts advise against asking customers about what they are most dissatisfied with in a company. They say it negatively affects the customers' attitudes and draws their attention to shortcomings. This is complete nonsense. When you let an unhappy person speak, sincerely acknowledge the issue he raises, and then do something to resolve it, his attention will shift away from the issue. In addition, it helps to prevent customers from sharing too much of their dissatisfaction with others.

«Your most unhappy customers are your greatest source of learning.» — Bill Gates, Microsoft co-founder

I recommend that you arrange it so that someone in your company regularly asks as many customers as possible, «From your point of view, what needs to be improved in our company?» Do not assign this task to salespeople; this information should be collected by a person who does not sell the company's products. If a salesperson conducts such surveys, the decline in his confidence in the company's products after conducting the survey will have a negative impact on revenues. The more beneficial a salesperson considers the company's products to be for the customer, the better he does at selling them. Do not undermine his confidence. Appoint someone else to conduct the surveys.

There is one more important point with regard to customer surveys. If while conducting the survey an employee were to come across a very dissatisfied customer, simple acknowledgement of the problem would not be enough. It would be important to resolve the issue the customer was dissatisfied with and compensate him for the inconvenience. Once, I took my car to a service station to have its suspension repaired. A week after the repair, I found that, from time to time, the car made a squeaking noise, which disappointed me, but I did not have enough time to take care of it. After a few days, I received a call from Jaguar to inquire about my satisfaction with the quality of the service I had received. I replied that I was dissatisfied and told them why. I was put through to an expert and I told him about my dissatisfaction. The expert very politely thanked me for the information I had provided, and that was all. No one from the company or from the service station ever called me about this issue again. A lot of time has passed since then. I have long since sold that car, but the bad impression remains.

Note that I am not saying that while creating a product you should try to please every customer. In many areas of business, that is simply impossible. In consulting, we cannot always provide customers with what they ask for. We have to provide them with what gives the best results. These are not necessarily the same thing. As an example, very often a business owner will come to my consulting company because of problems with his sales department. However, my experience tells me that the source of the problem is usually not in sales, but in advertising and other functions of the company. Either we have to succeed in convincing the owner that the entire company needs to be turned around (as opposed to simply asking for more effectiveness from the salespeople) or we will not accept this business owner as a customer. You may not agree with this approach, but I have reason to assert it. Look at how many businesses that you, as a customer, patronize. They are not trying to convince you to buy anything at all, yet they have lots of customers. If you disagree, just go to an Apple store. Recently, I went to the Apple store on Fifth Avenue in New York. Due to the time difference and the jet lag I experienced, I could not sleep. (Besides, walking around Manhattan on a summer night is a pleasure, since the streets are not as crowded and it is not so hot.) This store is open 24/7. I entered it at 4:00 a.m. to buy a laptop case. There were six sales assistants in the store. One of them helped me to find a case with a transparent cover, exactly what I wanted. Do you think he was trying to sell me something? He answered my questions, processed my order, brought the product, and that was all. It did not require any sales skills or techniques. At the same time, this is one of the largest computer stores in the world in terms of sales volumes and profits.

In sales, there is an opinion that the more you please customers, the more they will buy. To some degree, that is true. However, this is a very time-consuming process and only a few people like doing it professionally. The desire to please works well only when you sell luxury products. There are high profits in this type of business, so you can afford to spend a lot of effort on one customer. Investing in product improvement is, in most cases, more rational and productive than investing in salespeople.

For example, there are many steak houses in the same price bracket in New York. One of them is Del Frisco's Grille, a beautiful restaurant in Rockefeller Center that serves good-quality steaks and wine. You can go to this restaurant at almost any time, and there is no dress code. They wouldn't even mind if you went in shorts. Then there is Smith & Wollensky, which is not easy to get into. If you haven't booked a table in advance, you have almost no chance of getting in. Moreover, without a suit jacket, you most likely will not be allowed to enter. Both of these are chain restaurants with locations in multiple cities and are in approximately the same price range. However, if you ask locals which one you should try, more people would recommend Smith & Wollensky. I do not think it has anything to do with the organization of the sales process, but, rather, a difference in the companies' products.

For me a good product is like a work of art. Experience shows that a good product is almost impossible to copy, because when someone copies, they simply try to imitate someone without realizing what it is that they are actually imitating. Imitation is a very primitive form of creation. Sometimes it is necessary as a first step, but without moving to the next creative level, a bad imitation will just elicit condescending smiles from customers, and strengthen the position of the original. Recently, a new fast-food chain, McFoxy, was introduced in Ukraine. They tried to copy McDonald's in every respect—from restaurant locations and the appearance of items on the menu to dining room design and employee uniforms. They even tried to copy McDonald's advertising. The only difference was that this chain used only chicken. When the first restaurant opened, I was very interested in this company, because I had never before seen such a diligent attempt to copy someone else's product. When I went to McFoxy, I looked at it primarily from a customer's perspective. If I had never been to the original restaurant chain they were copying, it might have worked. But the attempted copy was different in almost every way: its speed of service, level of employee skills, cleanliness, and taste of the food. They were not able to copy anything to even a minimally acceptable degree, and the result was a huge difference from the original. In addition, some marketing «expert» had advised them to open their restaurants near McDonald's locations. In my opinion, this was a catastrophic mistake. They definitely should not have done it. If you are ever in Kiev, you will see two of these places for comparison right across from the railroad station. Definitely go there to see that a copy will never be better than the original, as aspirations to do or be «the same as they are» can only lead to «not as good.» I only hope that the owners of this company will eventually find their own path and we will all hear about their success. By the way, on the McFoxy web site it says, «McFoxy is the first entirely Ukrainian fast-food chain. Our employees' sincere smiles, fast service, welcoming atmosphere, and the best dishes at affordable prices always wait for you here. We are always happy to see you!» The only parts of this that are true is that they're an entirely Ukrainian chain and have affordable prices. The rest is just a slogan. I want to point out, though, that customers do not care whether they are a Ukrainian, Russian, or a foreign company. Customers want to receive a particular product, of a particular quality, at a particular price.

Packaging

An important part of any product is its packaging. The word *packaging* means completely different things depending on the business involved. To a fast-food chain, it means the appearance of the whole restaurant, its menu, and the dishes being served. To a paint-manufacturing company that sells its products at DIY stores, it means cans, boxes, and labels. To a consulting company, it means the appearance of its office, employees, and the documents it produces. To a distribution company, it means the appearance of its sales representatives, trucks, and documents.

As a rule, a customer does not perceive a product separately from its packaging, regardless of whether it has some functional purpose or not. A customer's desire to have a product depends on the appearance of its packaging, and the attention paid by customers to the product depends on the packaging's aesthetics. The value of attention has been previously discussed in this book. Unsightly images repel attention, and beautiful ones attract it. You could make a sandwich that tastes delicious, but if it looks ugly, you would have a difficult time trying to sell it. Of course, products that look good but are of poor quality are also considered a deception by customers.

Notice that in a supermarket you pay attention to two types of products: those you are already familiar with and those that attract your attention. Therefore, for the growth of a company and its market penetration, it is especially important to have an aesthetically pleasing product. Packaging, as a rule, serves to create or emphasize the aesthetics of a product. Try placing a lovely perfume in a plain medicine bottle; shoppers would get the impression that the contents would not smell very good. Just how aesthetically pleasing and attention-grabbing is your product? Do you use every opportunity to make it more aesthetically pleasing?

In 2001, Geroldmaster faced a problem with their packaging. Although the company was producing products that were wonderful in terms of their appearance, they were being shipped in large cardboard boxes. Each box contained thousands of medals that were packaged individually in small zipper bags. These product shipments looked just horrible. Moreover, customers complained that if they had to receive and stock a large number of medals, they were difficult to count this way. In order to resolve this issue, we developed small cardboard boxes that could contain about one hundred medals, then began to ship our products in them. These boxes turned out to be of such high quality and so aesthetically pleasing that many customers reused them for storage after their initial purpose was fulfilled. These boxes were used for a long time, helping to attract attention to our company's product. It is strange that such a simple idea did not come to the minds of any of our competitors.

When we at Visotsky Consulting needed to design and produce a package for the submission of paperwork and materials to our clients, we approached this matter very seriously. As a result, our corporate package takes up little space, is attractive, and, most important for me, can easily carry about eighteen pounds of documents. Our corporate notepads turned out to be so useful that many customers continued using them even a year after the completion of our consulting program. Thus, these customers promote our company to their colleagues. I want to point out that we designed several different versions of our notepads until we found the ideal form. Now we have only to make sure that no one tries to improve upon it and thereby ruin a good product.

The aesthetic form of a product consists of little details that create the entire look. The sensation people feel when touching the packaging of a product can significantly enhance or detract from the impression it makes. Packing paper that is too stiff, boxes that are impossible to open without a knife, bags with handles that are falling apart, documents that fall untidily all over the place, an unprofessional appearance of the office and employees — all of these things create a perception of low quality. It can be said that a product is complete when its form as well as its substance are perfect.

The more intangible your product is, the more attention you have to pay to its packaging. The less it differs from competitors' products, the more distinct its packaging should be. Banks' products, for example, can be considered one of the most intangible products. Banks provide you with money-management services, but they do not provide you with any guarantees of safety for your money above $250,000 in anyone account in the United States. That is interesting, is it not? We entrust banks with our money solely based on the idea that they are capable of handling it well, yet we do not receive any material guarantees above a certain threshold. Banks must inspire confidence — particularly after the debacle of the 2007 near collapse of the banking system. Therefore, packaging of bank services has to be perfect: Offices should look professional, employees should dress appropriately, and what the customer sees from his or her bank either in printed form or online should be crisply and clearly worded and presented. Also, the bank should have as many conveniently located offices as well as ATMs as possible, and the bank's logo should be widely displayed. If you want both your company and product to have credibility, it is important to create and maintain a perfect appearance for your company.

As an owner, you should not oversee the quality of your product and its appearance. This is a manager's function. However, the process of establishing standards for the product and its packaging is your direct responsibility, since you are the one who establishes a product's purpose and the product is a physical result of that purpose. This does not mean you need to be a designer, process engineer, or some other narrowly focused specialist. You can hire these experts and engage consultants, but you are the one responsible for making the entire company understand exactly what its product is and what the standards for the product are. Development of a strong foundation for brand formation is a part of this responsibility.

Brand

Formation of a successful brand always begins with a successful product. People will not care how attractive your company logo is if they do not understand and do not support your product. The idea behind creating a brand is that people can identify your successful product among similar products produced by competitors. If the product is mediocre, then sharp branding alone will just entrench its mediocrity in customers' minds and they will correctly reject this product when there is a choice. That is why putting a lot of effort into brand development and promotion without putting effort into product improvement is just a waste of money.

If your product is really good, it is necessary to design a recognizable logo and packaging, to describe in a brand book[16] the standards for the use of the logo, and to register a trademark so that in the future no one can copy the look of your product and its packaging and draw customer attention through deceit. You will also have to be diligent about ensuring that the standards created for use of the brand logo are correctly applied in practice so that the correct shapes, colors, and fonts are used. This is not an easy job! But if you do this successfully for a long time, the product will become more recognizable and will become easier and easier to market and sell. Now ask yourself, How easy would this be to do for a company with multiple products, each with different characteristics, levels of quality, and benefits for customers?

Brand management is also one of the business owner's functions.

---

[16] A brand book presents a set of rules for using a brand logo. It is a manual for the use of the brand in various communications. It regulates its use, protecting it from being used inappropriately by anyone.

Chapter 10

....

Company Policy

After the purpose of a company has been clearly defined and begins to be realized, a number of situations may arise, the correct resolution of which will determine the success of the implementation of the purpose. Company employees need to know how to act in various circumstances. They will not always make the right decisions if they rely solely on the purpose of the company. This is what company policy[17] is for.

Company policies are sets of rules to be followed by employees. If such rules don't exist, managers will have to give many individual instructions and orders in order to keep the purpose of the company from becoming distorted. The purpose of a company can be compared to a path that leads to the main goal of the company. Company policies represent walls along the sides of this path that protect the company from deviating from its intended purpose.

For example, if in the 1980s Steve Jobs had, in order to protect Apple's purpose, established a rule that the company would not license its operating system and would install it only on Apple computers, then Apple clones would not have been produced over a period of several years, thereby threatening Apple's existence. As a result, Apple would not have had to bear the expense of purchasing one of these clone manufacturers, Power Computing, in order to return Apple's operations to their intended purpose. If Geroldmaster had not established a policy of designing only medals and accepting orders for internal manufacturing only, then from time to time there would have been attempts to deviate from our purpose. If banking institutions didn't have the rule «Don't air your dirty laundry in public,» some occasions of fraud by bank employees would have been made public in the press. As a result, public confidence in the banks would have been damaged, and the harm would have been exacted not just on the particular banks involved but on the entire banking system. Please

---

[17] Company policy: a set of rules that provide general guidance for actions and decision making and contribute to the achievement of goals. A company policy makes clearer how goals need to be achieved. Within these rules, the policy allows freedom of action.

note, the banking sector is a huge field of activity that employs a large number of people. Given the sheer number of people employed in the banking system, the occasions of larceny and fraud are inevitable. Even so, you will most likely never read about the majority of these incidents in the press, as banking institutions have rules concerning the publicity of such incidents.

When you create and grow your company, there will be many issues for which you will need policies. Which issues should you tackle first when making these policies? Where should you begin? The most successful action here would be to monitor the operations of your business and create policies for those deviations that actually occur. There is no need to make anything up. Your observations will tell you which aspect of the company's operations need policies.

Other than just correcting deviations, company policies can also help to reinforce successful actions. One of our customers, an owner of a company that sells polyethylene, once asked me how to organize preparations for an exhibition to achieve maximum results. Each year, his company participated in a trade fair and ordered a well-equipped stand that attracted a lot of attention (which, naturally, was not a minor expense). I did not have a good handle on how to operate such an event, but I was able to help the company's executives recall what had worked successfully in past years; then I put that information together and developed a plan that would regulate operations during the exhibition. The document provided details on the times and locations where employees were supposed to be during their shifts at the stand, exactly what they were supposed do, how they should register visitors at the stand, what information they should collect, how their results would be quantitatively measured, what the stand supervisor was supposed to do, and what his authority was. Our team explained these rules to the employees who were assigned to work at the stand and conducted training sessions on their responsibilities. We spent less than two days doing this, but according to the reviews I received after the exhibition was over, it was the company's most productive exhibition ever. Even competitors told the company's owner how much they admired his stand's performance. Naturally, after the exhibition was over, it was reasonable to conduct some analysis of the results, make adjustments to the plan, and add to it some things that were initially missed. But even in its original first-run version, it had allowed for a significant increase in returns on effort and money spent. The point I want to emphasize here is that the plan consisted simply of those successful actions that executives already knew about.

Often we find that over time some very successful processes are forgotten. For various reasons, they are discarded. Then when the situations for which the successful processes were originally created are encountered again, they are brought back to mind. If you tried right now to recollect those company processes that were successful a long time ago but have since been forgotten, you would discover lots of interesting information. Here is a classic example. When your company was small and you needed to find your first employees, where did you turn? You asked your acquaintances and friends. Very often the people you found during that period became the core of your company for a long time. This is easy to explain: «Like attracts like» when it comes to people. Your friends and acquaintances are usually congenial souls, and their friends and acquaintances are generally close to you in spirit, as well. Then your company started to expand. As time went by, the company became larger. A number of new employees began working at the company and your original, very successful method of finding employees was forgotten. When Geroldmaster grew to employ over one hundred people, we began experiencing difficulties in hiring enough blue-collar workers. Anyone who has worked in manufacturing nowadays knows that it is easier to find a good manager than a skilled machine operator. I began to recall forgotten memories of previously successful actions. At every staff meeting, I encouraged employees to recruit their friends, announcing job vacancies and offering bonuses to those who recruited a friend (bonuses paid only upon successful completion of a probationary period, of course). After I saw how successful this was, I created a policy for the Human Resources Department so that this tool for recruiting employees' friends and acquaintances could be successfully applied throughout the company.

Sometimes I encounter a strange practice used by business consultants who help their clients formulate the main goal and purpose of their company. After formulating the main goal and purpose, they immediately try to write the main points of the company's policies. As a result, they get something like «We always deliver what we promise,» «Our customers are always satisfied,» «We always provide customers with more than promised,» and so on. To me, this sounds flat and uninspiring, for the simple reason that it is a completely typical approach to any business. You will rarely meet a person who does not share these same principles, so why write them down? We do not list in our policies such things as «Our employees should not steal, kill, or set the office on fire,» right? If you expend your efforts to set policy, it makes sense to pay attention to the things that are truly important. Pay attention to those areas where significant mistakes are usually made. Do not write a policy statement that says «There have to be satisfied customers.» It would be much better if you analyzed what makes your customers feel satisfied or dissatisfied, then write a policy that will lead to the desired results.

Near one of our offices is a restaurant that serves its food buffet-style. You take a tray, go along the counter, on which are different dishes, and take food yourself or with the help of the staff. The restaurant is not bad; the food is decent, the choice of dishes is enough for a business lunch, and the price is attractive. There is only one *but.* At the end of the counter, there is only one cash register, which on most days cannot handle the flow of people. I am usually able to finish eating a salad while waiting in line before I get to the register. On several occasions, I have seen a shift manager with a pained expression on his face standing next to the cashier, strenuously trying to help her serve customers more quickly.

These guys have a problem. They lose at least 50 percent of potential revenue during lunchtime because they cannot serve customers quickly enough. Many customers, disappointed with the speed of the service, have simply stopped going there for lunch. The only thing that saves the restaurant is that there are very few alternatives nearby. If they operated like this in Manhattan, they would have gone bankrupt long ago. The fact is, the purpose of a buffet service always contains the important element of speed. This only makes sense. If an owner really watches over the company's purpose, she or he will quickly find the obstacles to its implementation that the executives cannot handle. I am sure the owner would then come up with some «genius» idea that he could pass down to the executives, who, in turn, would offer some policy to deal with the problem.

Take a look at your company. What catches your eye as a deviation from your viewpoint on how the purpose should be implemented? Trust yourself. If something draws your attention, it is usually very important. To test how important something is, ask yourself, What does this have to do with the purpose of my company?

You do not necessarily have to write each policy yourself. Record your main ideas on tape, hand it to the executive responsible for the area the policy will cover, and tell him or her to draft a policy. Do not allow too much time for your manager to write one, since the draft will probably be written in the last three hours of the allotted time anyway. Then you just have to verify it, add your comments, and it is almost finished.

One hot summer day while one of my executives was delivering a report, I realized that my attention was not focused on what she was saying. Instead, it was fixed on how her skirt was defying gravity and staying on her hips. It was a year when low-slung skirts that displayed the wearer's midriff were in fashion. After the meeting, I began to pay more attention to what the employees were wearing around the office. I found that many of our female employees came to work dressed in a manner that was not appropriate for a business environment. I had Human Resources write rules that would include both male and female dress codes for office and manufacturing employees, rules for the use of makeup and perfumes, and hot weather dress codes. Then I only had to approve the rules for this policy and endorse their implementation in the company.

I chose this example because the attire worn by employees is a very common issue in small to medium-size businesses. Certainly this won't be the first policy issue you address. Perhaps you should begin with pricing and discounting policies, or product quality–control policies, or something else that is a priority for your company. It is important for you to understand that company policies are your responsibility. The fewer rules you have, the more hands-on management you will have to perform and the more you will have to give verbal instructions and orders, and oversee their execution.

Creation of policies on really important issues forms a strong framework the entire organization can build on. As the old Buddhist proverb says, «During good times, a good man reinforces traditions so that during bad times the traditions strengthen him.»

As you begin to shape the policies of your company, you will find that it is not that easy. That is why I am giving you two pieces of advice that will help you. The first piece of advice concerns the form of company policies. Whether employees will want to follow a policy, and thus how much effort you will have to exert in order to enforce it, will depend on the form of the policy. Here are the seven basic points that should be included in a policy document:

1. The source of the policy document (who issued it.)
2. The title of the document and its publication date/ revision date.
3. The job positions to which this policy applies.
4. A description of the specific issue this policy aims to address.
5. Examples that demonstrate that a problem really does exist and what will result if the problem continues.
6. A description of the rule or principle that employees should follow to address the issue.
7. The end result of compliance with these rules.

More detail on the above points:

1. As your company grows, you, the owner, will not be the only one to create policies; divisional and departmental executives will also be involved in their creation. Naturally, however, the policies created by the owner are the «constitution» of the company, and no policies issued by executives can go against the policies of the owner. That is why it is important to indicate the source of the policy. For example, the source of the policy can refer to the «Office of the Owner» or «Chief Executive» or «Director of Human Resources.» In this way, if a contradiction arises, employees can determine which rules takes precedence.

2. The title of the document should be easy to remember and reflect its content. For example, if you publish a policy regarding a system of discounting, then simply name the document «System of Discounting.» Be sure to specify the date of initial publication and the date of the latest revision, as it is certain that particular statements and rules in policy documents will need to be revised as time goes by. In such cases, it is necessary to withdraw the old versions and provide the new ones to employees. However, during the time the older version of a policy was in use, it may have been referenced in various instructions and documents. In order not to have to reissue all of these related documents and collapse the working system, leave the title and the initial date of publication the same, but state the date of the latest revision.

3. List all of the positions or groups of positions to which this particular policy applies. If it applies to all employees (rules of conduct, dress code, etc.), then just indicate «To All Employees.»

4. Describe the issue to be addressed by the policy. This is necessary in order to show employees that there is indeed something that needs to be resolved. For example, let us look at the policy for a dress code at work. There are employees in your company who dress professionally even without any formal rules; it is natural to them. When they are handed this policy, they may be confused, since they were unaware of this dress code problem until you told them about it. These employees may even think that management simply has nothing better to do than to «fix what isn't broken.»

5. To make the problem more vivid and real, give examples. Do not state any names in your examples, particularly if the examples are negative. There is no need to immortalize your employees' mistakes and create a bad name for them.

6. There should be a description of the rule being instituted. Describe it in as simple language as possible. For some strange reason, when people write official documents, they often express them in some confusing or convoluted language. Instead of writing «Never press the red button,» they may write «An employee should not put the device into operation via activation of the red switch.» The simpler the language you use to describe necessary actions, the less effort will be required to execute them. An executive of a boiler-manufacturing enterprise once asked me, «Recently one of our factories was certified as ISO 9001:2008[18]-compliant, but is it really possible to make this standard work in reality, not just on paper?» I asked him to provide me with the regulatory documents that described the responsibilities of employees with regard to quality management according to the ISO standard. It took me a lot of time to read the documents, as they were written in a completely incomprehensible scientific language with heaps of technical terms. There was really no need for that. I concluded that it would be easy enough to meet the requirements set forth in the document if they were translated into plain English. Some consultants just can't help unnecessarily complicating things. Perhaps it is because they are afraid of being unemployed. But whatever the reason, it was impossible to ensure that an industrial worker from a small village in Ukraine, where the factory was located, could understand these documents. As a result, this simple and good ISO standard did not work in spite of all the money spent on the development of documents and staff training.

Sometimes business owners ask me what qualities a person who helps them write policies should have. The first quality that comes to my mind is that he or she should be able to explain any idea in simple language. By the way, the ability to use simple language, or «dumb down» an explanation of some principle, demonstrates a person's level of ability.

7. Describe what advantages the company would gain, what the win in operations would be, and define the benefit. If you can also manage to mention the main goal or purpose here, that would be just wonderful.

---

[18] ISO 9001:2008 Quality Management Systems Requirements: one of the standards developed by ISO (International Organization for Standardization). The standard itself does not regulate a product's quality, but establishes requirements for the system governing the process control and improvement of quality. It is safe to say that the compliance with the standard's requirements indicates a certain level of reliability of a company as a supplier of its product.

Don't forget to sign the document. Even if it was written by one of your executives, you should, without any hesitation, remove any traces of his or her authorship and publish the document under your name. This is very important. From my personal experience, I have found that when I left the information about the real author of a policy in place, instead of executing the required rules, employees began to discuss the document from the point of view of whether the author of the document was competent enough to write it. This led to failure in implementing the policy. Policies work much better when employees know that it was established by an owner, and that is why it needs to be implemented, not discussed and assessed.

So, you've written (or had some executive write) the company's policies. My second piece of advice for you is how to enforce the policies that you have approved.

We all like it when the handbooks and manuals we need to work with are within reach, instead of our having to go to another office every time we need one. The same applies to policies. If you want your employees to know and follow them, they should always be conveniently available. That is why you need to arrange it so that every employee has at their desk a folder in which to file all new policies related to their position in the company. Spare neither folders nor paper. They are not so expensive that an employee should have to run to some other location to order to find out how they should act in a particular situation. I'm amused when some owners ask me, «Why does every employee need an individual folder if I have several salespeople who fulfill the same functions?» I want to respond by asking, «Why do you need a personal computer if all the executives can use the same one?» It doesn't matter if the person is a high-powered executive, a machine operator, or a janitor; the individual should still have a folder that contains all of the company policies related to his or her position.

As soon as a new policy statement is filed in an employee's folder, the employee's knowledge of it should be tested. You'll find that most employees file their copy without reading it. It is commonplace; that is why you need to test them. Ask questions that an employee will be able to answer only if he or she has read the policy. Employees who cannot answer your questions should be given time to study and then be retested later. The only way to get people to know the policies is to test them. There are no other effective ways. I have checked.

Other than making copies of policies, distributing them to employees, and testing them, you should carefully store the originals of these documents and put together folders for new employees (when a new employee is first appointed to a position, there are some policy documents for that position already). Human Resource departments usually handle this, which is why an owner should be vitally concerned that this department functions well. Otherwise, it will be difficult to provide the company with working policies.

The greater the number of smart, targeted policies you publish to solve important issues, the thicker the employees' folders become and the more regulated and streamlined the company's operations will be. The orientation process for new employees becomes easier, and is easier to manage. Of course, the higher the employee is in the company's hierarchy, the thicker his policy folder will be. A senior or middle manager should know perfectly every detail of the policies that regulate his subordinates' actions.

Chapter 11

Technology

Every type of business has its own technology for producing its product. Even a shoe retailer has exact methodologies for selecting the styles for a collection and determining the quantity and sizes of each style that will be ordered. There are special techniques to help sell more shoes, and techniques to determine whether a particular shoe style suits a particular person or not. If you have a manufacturing facility, there are exact ways to perform various processes in order to manufacture a product that meets your company's standards.

When the technology of a business is not defined but is available only at the fingertips of a few experts in the company, you cannot truly call it a business, because it is impossible to expand operations. To expand, a company must be able to train more employees and oversee the quality of its production process. In addition, the company's success will be fully dependent on those few individuals who know the technology, and the company as a whole will be at the mercy of these few people. If you, the owner, happen to be one of those individuals, then you will unable to break out of the daily routine and be fully engaged in the business owner's role until you define your knowledge and transfer it to others.

In 2003, while in the medal-manufacturing business, for the first time I encountered a problem with the organization of our production area. Thanks to the good quality of our products and our successful promotion of them, we started to receive a large number of orders. However, our manufacturing unit was unable to plan accurately for such high-volume production, as for this kind of planning the individuals involved needed to know exactly what technical processes each product needed to go through, what equipment would be used, what the complexity of each process was, and what level of qualification the operator performing the process should possess. Without these accurate descriptions of our technological processes, those who were responsible for production planning was like running in circles. We would create a plan for the week, then have to change it every day. The production and supply divisions were sent into a tailspin, and those working in these areas of the company were in a constant state of stress. The sales department was frantic, as well, for it could not provide customers with accurate information on lead times for orders.

We were able to overcome this problem only after we found a consultant who defined for us all of our technological processes, standard production times, and the equipment and materials needed for manufacturing each product. We had to establish skill-set levels for various types of operations and assign all of the factory employees to these different levels according to their qualifications. Only after completing this process were we able to change our production planning so that schedules were accurately estimated and manufacturing could meet them. Fortunately, in this company I was not one of the individuals who had in-depth knowledge of our technology, nor was I even a good technician. Therefore, as soon as I became aware that this problem existed, I was immediately able to begin looking for someone who could describe the technology of our manufacturing process step by step to me. It turned out not to be very difficult to find such a person, as there were already a number of specialized institutes in this field in the country. The most important thing was for me to understand what I wanted to achieve as the result of this expertise.

Successful technology has great value. This is one reason why franchises like McDonald's flourish. What Ray Kroc sold to people who wanted to open a restaurant under the McDonald's trademark was actually technology. At the dawn of the creation of this chain, the description of the restaurant's operating technology fit into just one brochure. Today, it takes thousands of pages to describe not only how to make hamburgers but all other operational aspects involved — from how to hire and train new employees to the responsibilities of restaurant executives.

Technology is an exact description of how to materialize a company's purpose. Therefore, when someone buys a franchise, which includes the technology for producing its product, he or she actually joins a purpose that has already been formulated and time-tested, and does not create one him or herself. In this case, the franchiser performs certain functions of the business owner: establishment of the main goal and purpose, creation of fundamental policies, creation of the product, and, certainly, development of the technology of the company.

«Nothing works better than just improving your product.» — Joel Spolsky, Stack Overflow confound

Why is the development of the technology the responsibility of the owner and not the company executives? Because in order to develop technology, one needs to be outside of the daily routine. In order to create rules and standards, it is necessary to, on the one hand, attentively observe operations and, on the other, not be too deeply absorbed in them. It is also necessary to have the opportunity and time to study the market conditions, new technologies, the activities of competitors, and the evolving preferences of customers. People involved in day-to-day production are usually so absorbed by the routine that they are unable to do this.

This is also the reason why the research and development (R&D) department should not be under the manufacturing division. When I was at Badge Master, a company that manufactured machines and devices for making badges and souvenirs, the company originally had its R&D department under its manufacturing division. Over time, as the company's production increased, we found two problems emerged as a result. The first was that the R&D department was continuously improving the machines the company produced, and, as a result, every batch of machines was different. This created a lot of problems in servicing these machines, as after a few years no one could tell which replacement parts fit which machines — a conundrum frustrated both customers and the employees. The second problem was that our cost of manufacturing these machines gradually and imperceptibly increased as the various improvements were introduced. Over time, the machines, which were supposed to be within certain price ranges, moved out of these ranges and thus became significantly less competitive than they had been initially. Badge Master solved these problems when it separated the R&D department from manufacturing and had R&D report directly to the owner. This way, the tasks for the R&D department were not set by manufacturing, or by sales, but by those who developed the product from the point of view of improving its position in the market. The same kind of problem could occur if a restaurant owner allowed the recipes and menu to be changed at the sole discretion of the chef. Depending on the chef's creativity and preferences, the restaurant could find itself drifting beyond its intended range of prices, essentially deviating from its purpose.

This does not mean that a chef should not have anything to do with selecting a restaurant's recipes and planning its menu. That would be impossible, and unnecessary. In fact, a chef performs two different functions. The first is to develop the technology of the restaurant's food preparation — which is part of the technology of the restaurant — under the direction of the business owner. He does this in order to improve the company's product and allow the business purpose to be more accurately implemented. The chef's second function is to manage the production process, whereby he achieves the highest quality of dishes, produced from the approved recipes.

A company's lead experts and experienced employees can and should be involved in the development of a company's technology. However, it is important to understand that while they are engaged in this function, they act as consultants and experts to the owner, and when they use this technology in their jobs, they have a completely different task, which is to produce a higher-quality product. The establishment of quality standards is part of technology development, and it helps to accurately define the quality level of a company's product. Take, for example, the café serving Iranian ethnic food, which I discussed in chapter 8. In addition to the foods served on the premises, the café also offers delivery of pies and other dishes that it makes. Along with its quality standards for the preparation of its national ethnic dishes, the café also has standards for the process of taking orders over the telephone and managing them so that quality and timely delivery are ensured.

You can get many good ideas on technology improvement when you observe how various businesses in the United States or abroad operate. When I am asked where to get good ideas for improving technology, I always recommend traveling to another area or country to observe how companies in the same industry operate there. Observe your competitors—not necessarily even the most successful ones. If you are observant enough, you will find that even the most mediocre competitor can offer something interesting in its operations processes. Of course, any new ideas should be tested before they become a part of your company's technology. This is why an owner keeps all pilot projects for new technologies under his control.

Nowadays, there are many companies that sell technologies. They happily provide presentations on their solutions and new products, but you must be careful with new products. Be sure they definitely work before you invest money and effort in them. If a company sells equipment that truly works, it can provide you with a tour of other companies that use its equipment and technology. Perhaps the companies in your area will not want to reveal all of their secrets, but you can always go to another area or abroad and learn from the experiences of other businesses there.

When you evaluate the possibility of introducing a new technology into your company, it is important to consider the matter from both the technological and organizational points of view. For example, in 2005 Hewlett-Packard actively promoted the Indigo series of digital printers to publishers. They claimed this equipment allowed users to print small, typographical-quality runs just as easily as printing on a regular printer. Many printing companies bought this rather expensive equipment because nearly all of them had problems with small print runs. When printing limited runs on standard sheet printers, their costs and prices were too high. However, very few of these printing companies could provide a sufficient workload for the new equipment to cover its costs, not to mention making a profit. The reason for this was simple: To fully load an Indigo machine, print orders had to arrive as fully completed work, ready for printing. An entire army of designers and coders were needed in order to provide and sustain enough short-run work to load the machine, and the amount of work done prior to the printing itself was so large that one such machine could service hundreds of advertising agencies. But the local ad agency market did not have the level of integration and cooperation needed to accomplish this. As a result, these wonderful modern machines were idle most of the time, and their owners did not know how to get rid of them. If you look at it from the company's ideological point of view, it becomes obvious that this equipment was not made for these printing companies. These machines were designed for a completely different business purpose—that of small, on-the-fly printing companies that service a number of advertising agencies, not end customers. That is why when a business owner makes decisions regarding new technologies for his company, he must ensure that all new ideas are accord with the company's purpose.

Chapter 12

....

The Strategic Management Cycle

«So often people are working hard at the wrong thing. Working on the right thing is probably more important than working hard.» — Caterina Fake, Flickr co-founder

Strategic management is the art of directing the operations of an organization toward the achievement of the organization's main goal. As mentioned in the earlier discussion on goals, strategic planning is not about the achievement of milestones, but about the meaning of a company's existence. Of course, this movement toward a company's main goal is carried out through the achievement of intermediate goals.

There is a perception in society that strategic management is used only by corporations and is out of reach and unnecessary for small businesses. But ask yourself if you want to expand your company to a size that really satisfies you. In order for a small company to achieve something worthwhile, it has to make the best use of its available resources. A large corporation can waste millions on a number of experiments, only one of which may be a success. But, as a rule, small businesses pay a high price for every strategic mistake they make. The cost may be a few years of marking time, or even a company's very survival.

Strategic management is a simple tool that allows you to achieve fast and controllable expansion. In fact, every business owner of a more or less stable business, no matter its size, will have already implemented some successful strategy. In a small business, it frequently happens that in the beginning there was a good idea, but having implemented it, the company stops growing. Look at how many small companies successfully provide outsourced accounting services. How many of them have become large? Or consider how many small companies successfully sell preowned cars. Very few have become big. There's no real reason for these companies dealing in preowned cars to remain small. They don't have complex and expensive technologies, and their market share can be considerable. There are a sufficient number of trained mechanics, lots of financing services available for purchasing vehicles, and this type of business doesn't require a significant investment. So what prevents these companies from attracting more and more customers and growing as large as CarMax? The same lack of growth is true with regard to successful restaurants, shops, and manufacturers. After learning how to provide high-quality products and starting to make money, they cannot expand. In order for a business to expand, someone has to work at it.

The strategic management cycle consists of two phases: planning what to do and then continuously overseeing the execution of the plans. There is only one snag: No strategy gets implemented within a week or a month; long-term oversight is required. Intention alone is not enough. Even implementing a single plan, like opening a new office in a neighboring region, requires the coordinated execution of a number of actions. It is necessary to obtain funding, rent space, hire and train staff, launch an advertising campaign, and so on. These actions are performed by various employees of the company. These same employees also have their regular jobs, which are also important, as the ability to expand usually relies upon the success of ongoing operations, since money is needed in order to expand. Therefore, during the oversight phase, a business owner has to ensure that operational problems don't bury growth plans.

It should be noted that during the oversight phase, your main ally as a business owner is the aspiration of the employees for improvement and advancement. The most capable segment of employees in a group want the company to grow stronger and expand, since this leads to their own attainment of a new, higher level. They are inspired by the future and the achievement of obtainable, challenging goals. It is something in which they take an active and deliberate role. Pay attention to the word *deliberate*. Very often, an owner may try to implement a plan and give his employees specific tasks to be performed. However, all of these employees are absorbed in their daily routines and don't understand or believe that these tasks lead to further achievements. They see them only as a hindrance to their current responsibilities. It's very easy to turn capable people into enemies of the company's growth: Just keep them in the dark about growth plans and don't explain to them why their tasks are important. Have you ever been forced to do something that you initially didn't see any reason for doing? Think of your attitude toward this task. I'll bet there was no enthusiasm at all. After a time, you might have found that eventually something like «Why the hell didn't they tell me why this needed to be done?» involuntarily escaped from your lips.

So when you, as the business owner, feel as if you alone are pushing the company up a mountain, recognize that this is the inevitable consequence of a lack of strategic management. Instead of getting support, you encounter resistance. When the resistance becomes too great, you may think that the people around you think only about today and don't even care about their own future. But in that moment, remember how these same people supported you during the times when they clearly understood the direction in which you were leading the company. This direction was especially clear when the company first began its operations. As I mentioned before, when first creating a company, the strategy is simple and clear: Start operations, learn customer service, and start making money. Sometimes, it may even seem to you that the existing staff is willing to accept only a simple strategy. But this is not the case. Put simply, this is the result of your being able to promote only a simple strategy. When it came time to take the next step for the company, you, the promoter of future goals, did not have enough determination or skill to inspire your employees for the next step in the company's growth.

Another important point relates to the fear of making mistakes. None of us is perfect; we all make mistakes. And when the person who establishes the goals makes a mistake, he or she can lead people down a blind alley. But do you know what's interesting? If a company doesn't advance, if it doesn't grow, it's already in a blind alley.

At some point, I was inspired by a topic I found in L. Ron Hubbard's works. It was his Tone Scale of Decisions[19].

Making decisions that can be put into effect

Making decisions that cannot be put into effect

Indecision

Irrational decision to force irrational decision into effect

Indecision

Decision not to be

When we face a new field of activity that isn't simple and natural to us (and people management is not something natural to humans), it takes some time to begin feeling comfortable in this new field. That's

---

[19] L. Ron Hubbard, «Decision,» Lecture in The Route to Infinity Lectures (Los Angeles: Golden Era Productions, 2003), 142–143.

why it's very rare for anyone to start their actions at the highest level of this scale. Usually, we begin to act in this new field at one of the lower levels—but certainly not at the lowest level, «Decision not to be.» On this level are people who have already lost their battle and have removed themselves from a position of management. These are people who look for magical solutions. They seek out people who will do everything for them, or use horoscopes to identify the favorable time to do something. They have completely renounced their independent decisions and compliantly follow the opinions of «experts.»

The first level up from the bottom is «Indecision.» Regarding business owners, people on this level realize that they need to establish a strategy but are in doubt as to whether they should assume the responsibility for it. I've met a lot of people like this. Some of them read various books and attend workshops, searching for reassurance that strategy is not their responsibility. They believe they finished their job as an owner when they started a business and that now it's time for the executives to shine. But their persistent search only confirms that they don't really believe this themselves and that somewhere deep down they know that this is their duty as an owner. This level is illustrated by the fact that there is no real action here, only doubt.

The next level up is the level of «Irrational decision to force irrational decision into effect.» In comparison to the previous level, this one is a breakthrough, as there is action here. On this level, a business owner behaves eccentrically and experiments. Unfortunately, these experiments involve people, which is not forbidden in the management field, although it is in the health-care realm. At the same time, this level is a turning point, as irrational decisions always lead to destructive consequences and disappointment that can push one further down the scale. I want to point out that a leader on this level is at least still alive, as he is able to insist on the implementation of his decisions. This person has enough energy but not enough knowledge to achieve what he wants. These are people who do things like try to create a popular online gourmet grocery store. People enjoy going to a gourmet grocer and choosing something tasty. They need to see, smell, and touch things. How can you choose a nice cut of steak or a delicious bakery item online? Nevertheless, a number of successful gourmet grocery stores have started projects to expand online instead of focusing their efforts on improving customer service or increasing the number of their stores.

Upon realizing that these unusual solutions don't work, but not having lost the desire to take action, these business owners may rise to the higher level of «Indecision.» This is a completely different kind of «Indecision» than the lower-level one. Here there is simply a lack of understanding of what to do and which growth path to choose. For these people, it becomes obvious what should not be done, but what should be done is still not understood by them.

On the next level up the scale, «Making decisions that cannot be put into effect,» there are decisions that are positive in their essence but are inadequate for the circumstances in which they are made. On the scale, these are decisions that are impossible to implement. So after reading a motivational book or participating in an inspiring workshop, an owner says, «We will become a global company. We will become the number-one company in». But he cannot answer the question of precisely how this will happen. This is similar to fanaticism, and there are always some not-too-bright people ready to believe it. The owner of a car-repair shop that performs good bodywork told me his repair shop would turn into an international chain. But when I asked him what his next steps toward this goal would be, he couldn't communicate anything concrete. He had wonderful dreams, and I hope they will come true. But this will happen only after he creates a feasible plan, and not before. Still I want to point out that this is quite a high level. In spite of often being laughed at behind their backs, these people are still closer to success than those who are at the lower levels of the scale. If you find yourself at this level, congratulations! The only thing you lack is the know-how to make a plan and implement it.

The highest level of the scale is about making decisions that can be carried out. This level of business owner either has some technique to create effective plans or is so talented that he doesn't need a technique to create them.

I hope I've rubbed enough salt in your wounds so that you now want to take on strategic management in your company. Here are the steps you as the business owner must do so that your decisions are reasonable and can be carried out.

The first thing you need to do is decide when your fiscal year will begin. This is far from being the most important step, but you can create a lot of extra problems for yourself if this is done incorrectly. At the end of a fiscal year, you take stock, formulate plans, and put together a plan of action. If you choose the calendar year as your fiscal year, then in December you'll need to do planning, conduct brainstorming sessions, and hold meetings with your top executives. But for many businesses, December is a period of increased activity, when management's workload also increases, and it will take considerable effort to get your executives to work on the company's strategy if you do it in December. In Japan, most companies begin their fiscal year on April 1.

Most companies in the United States begin their fiscal year on October 1. Microsoft begins its fiscal year on July 1. If a business is seasonal, it's a good practice to begin the fiscal year in the month preceding the start of a season. So if the season in your business starts in March, it's better to conduct strategic planning in February. Certainly none of this is reason to wait until the off-season to begin planning. If you've never done strategic planning before, start as soon as possible. Every month wasted is a month of routine, and even more important, it's one less month to experience the pleasure derived from the achievement of your goals.

The strategic management cycle, which you should conduct at least once a year (for small companies it is better to do it at least every six months), consists of a few simple steps. A few years ago, I read about these steps in a series of articles on strategy by L. Ron Hubbard. I describe the owner's responsibilities with regard to each step, as well as what is needed from the company's executives. Here are the basic steps that must be undertaken at least every six months to a year:

1. Updating the main goal and purpose statement of the company
2. Identifying the greatest obstacle or obstacles to the company's growth
3. Forming the main idea of the strategic plan or plans
4. Writing the strategic plans
5. Writing up the projects that correspond to the approved strategic plans
6. Overseeing the execution of the projects

The first step of the strategic management cycle is updating the company's main goal and purpose. Imagine that it has been a year since you established the company's main goal and purpose. Over that time, you've had new experiences, you've observed a lot, and you have repeatedly told your employees about the company goals. Quite possibly, during that time you yourself saw something new with regard to the goals, some new aspects. Certainly the base stays the same, but when you talk about something important repeatedly, over time the wording becomes even clearer. That is why at this step, simply taking the current wording of the main goal and purpose of the company and looking at it as if you were seeing it for the first time is important. Then make any necessary changes and distribute the updated document to every employee in the company. In addition to doing this, you'll want to announce the changes during the next staff meeting and explain what prompted you to make them.

If you've been engaged in strategic planning for a while, then you might leave the main goal and purpose as they are. This would mean that your wording was already well defined, and there was no need to change anything. Even if you do decide to change something, it will take only a couple of hours of your time. This step may seem like a mere formality, but it is not. Any change made to the wording of your main goal and purpose influences all of the steps that follow. For example, suppose the initial wording of your main goal was «to make the life of our city's residents more comfortable.» Now suppose that over time you've found that the main comfort your company creates for customers is the extra free time your services allow them. You might, therefore, change the wording of the main goal to something different, such as «to make the lives of our city's residents freer, because they will have more time to pursue their interests.» Will this change influence the company's operations, its strategy, and its standards? Undoubtedly. True, these changes will take place only when the goal is understood and accepted by your employees. Sometimes these challenges will make you work hard.

The second step is the least technical yet most difficult of all the steps of the strategic management cycle. For this step, you need to look at the company's operations from a bird's-eye view. You need to gather information on how the company's quantitative indicators have changed over the past year, how the market situation and customers' needs have changed, what your competitors have done, and which strategic objectives your company has achieved over this period. You need to look at the company from the outside. This isn't easy to do if you, the owner, are caught up in the daily routine of the business. As a result of this step, you need to identify the biggest obstacles to your company's growth. Ideally, the biggest one.

A strategic plan begins with the observation of a situation[20] to be handled or a goal to be met.[21]

You might have wondered why some companies grow rapidly while others freeze in their growth, even when they have an excellent product, or why some people achieve a lot in life and others just drag out a miserable existence. Working harder is not the determining factor. You'd agree that a janitor does not work significantly less than the owner of a prosperous company. When we were children we were taught to work hard and were told that hard work would lead

---

[20] In this instance, «situation» means a major departure from the ideal scenario. See (L. Ron Hubbard, «The Situation,» in The Management Series, vol. 1 (Los Angeles: Bridge Publications, 2001), 507.

[21] L. Ron Hubbard, «Strategic Planning,» in The Management Series, vol. 1 (Los Angeles: Bridge Publications, 2001), 283.

to success. But this isn't true. Hard work is undoubtedly admirable and brings certain satisfaction, but achievement of bigger goals brings even more satisfaction. A key factor in goal achievement is not how persistent you are, but *what* you do. If a janitor works several times harder than his colleagues, he will still not be able to become head of the company, will not be able to buy a big house, and will not be able to send his kids to a prestigious university. This is why it is important to first understand what needs to be done and what is a priority, and only then should you begin to work persistently to achieve the goal.

Let's return again to my client who owns the wonderful café serving Iranian ethnic cuisine. I have lunch there whenever I get the chance. Nowhere else have I eaten such delicious soups and pies. Only my grandmother could make something similar. The excellent cuisine, good service, and pleasant decor of the café attract a large number of customers. For this reason, it's difficult to dine there in the afternoon. But the problem is that the café is on the fifth floor of a mall, and it's the only restaurant on that floor. In addition, the mall opens late and closes early, especially on weekends. As a result, the café misses out on the most profitable times for restaurants, which are evenings from Friday through Sunday. Due to its poor location the café loses at least half of its potential revenues. If you examine the operations of the café from the perspective of the owner, you could identify a number of drawbacks. There are always problems with the staff, kitchen, or service quality. But there is one problem that is significantly larger and more important than any other: the location of the café. If strategic planning is not directed toward fixing this particular problem, the results of any other efforts exerted will be minimal.

Another example is a company that manufactures polypropylene[22] thermal insulation. In a conversation I had with the owner, he lamented that the seasonality of his business required him to hire additional workers at the beginning of the season and then lay them off during the off-season. These workers had to be trained each season before they became sufficiently competent, and before they were fully trained, they produced a lot of defective material and also bungled shipments. In addition, his company always failed to hire enough people in time for the season, so when the season started, the company unable to fulfill all of the customers' orders quickly, and some business was lost to competitors. The owner had tried to find a way to train new employees more quickly and design some additional products that would be in

---

[22] Polypropylene is a smooth-surface plastic that cracks easily when bent but is difficult to scratch; it is used in making battery cases, jar lids, margarine tubs, straws, etc.

demand during the off-season. During the off-season, the company didn't make enough money to cover its costs. In addition to the high cost of overhead and expenses during the off-season, there was also the problem of how to keep the remaining staff busy. In this example, the biggest obstacle for the company was not the training of employees nor keeping them occupied, but the seasonal production fluctuations of the business.

A method that works well to identify the main problem in a company is to ask «Why?»

Question: Why is it that we cannot quickly hire a sufficient number of employees at the beginning of a season?
Answer: During this period, the demand for construction professionals increases.

Question: Why can't we quickly train the people we hire?

Answer: The most talented professionals already have jobs, and those who are looking for a job at the beginning of a season are not the best.

Question: Why do we look for people and train them at the beginning of a season?

Answer: Because we cannot provide year-round employment for them.

Question: Why can't we provide them with year-round employment?

Answer: Because we cannot work just to produce inventory.

Question: Why can't we work just to produce inventory?

Answer: We do not have a sufficient stock of raw materials or working capital.

Question: Why don't we have sufficient working capital?

Answer: We cannot accumulate enough capital due to a lack of high profitability, and the off-season eats up what little savings we do amass.
It becomes obvious that we've arrived at the main *why*. The answer

is a lack of working capital. Now, let's test it to see if it is truly the main question. If we had enough working capital for raw materials and could work year-round, then during the off-season we could work to produce inventory, and during the season we could work to fulfill orders. Is that possible? Yes, it is, because the product range includes a line of standard panels that are frequently used in construction. Of course, the mobilization of working capital has its price and creates certain risks, which is why it is worth assessing what is gained and what is lost with this approach.

My experience tells me that the real problems that stall a company's growth are always very, very simple. It is quite probable that the owner of this company had contemplated the idea of operating year-round and warehousing some of its products for part of each year. So why, then, didn't he work out a plan to implement it? The answer is simple. In this decision, there is something he doesn't want to face. You see, for years he has worked with customers who place orders in advance, and he's accustomed to this particular approach—so much so that he cannot overcome this habit. Habits are phenomenal things, especially if a habit has brought success at one point or even over a long period of time. Ten years before, this businessman created a company that manufactured products to order. At that time, profitability was high enough, the competition was weak, and this model of operation was sufficient to make profits and achieve growth. In addition, his ambitions were much more modest. Times changed, but the habit stayed the same. There is even a special term for this. It is called «being stuck in a victory.» I often meet people who while in this state lose their ability to see what is really going on around them. Perhaps ten years earlier it wasn't possible for him to mobilize additional working capital, or maybe there were some other obstacles he could not overcome. But it was okay because things were good at that time. Today's situation is significantly different, yet he continues to ignore that.

While working in the consulting industry, I have found an effective way to force an owner to overcome his habits and face his problems. It just requires an honest assessment of what the gains and losses would be for the company to implement a solution to the problem, and then compare those to the cost of not implementing the solution. In this case, the company needed to consider the loss of potential sales at the beginning of a season, the costs of recruiting and training new staff each season, the costs of layoffs at the end of a season, off-season losses, and the costs of equipment preservation. It all came to a hefty sum. The company then needed to compare this to the cost of mobilizing additional working capital and covering additional warehouse expenses. When we calculated all of that, the owner was shocked at how much money his company had lost over the past few years. As soon as he this became clear to him, I had to keep him from rushing out to handle the situation immediately. I wanted him first to work out a proper plan, and only then start to take action. Interestingly, as soon as he could quantitatively assess the size of the problem, he instantly started coming up with great ideas on how to get money for the purchase of raw materials and where to find a cheap warehouse.

Therefore at this step, I recommend carefully looking at your company's operation and asking the question «Why is this happening?» Don't accept that there are a number of various reasons. There is always one problem that is the largest which, once resolved, will allow you to really further the growth of your company. A monetary evaluation of the costs imposed by the existing state of affairs will give you more courage. This is not because money is most important—not at all. Money simply serves as a tool with which to measure the value of various things. So use it accordingly—as a measure.

Another important skill in determining the most important problem is the ability to ignore everything minor. Of course, an owner has a lot of day-to-day issues: technological developments, sales levels, discipline, labor capacity, and many others. If you get distracted by various issues and don't focus all of your efforts on solving the most important one, the company will continue putting out fires and its growth will remain only in your dreams.

It's very tempting to begin looking for a solution immediately after identifying a problem. Try to keep yourself and others from doing this. You'll create a solution in the next (third) step. The formation of a solution is a creative process that's really exciting, but it's necessary to keep yourself from coming up with a solution until you are sure you are on the right path. At this step of identifying the main obstacles to your company's growth, you, as the owner, play the most important role. This doesn't mean that you shouldn't involve your top-level executives in this. However, I recommend that you first identify the obstacle (or obstacles) for yourself and make sure that you've identified the most important one or ones before getting others involved. You will find that the executives usually cannot identify the most important issue facing the company because their point of view is from the inside. They're used to working with a certain system and will look only for deviations from that system. You are the creator of the system, and it is therefore easier for you to see the larger picture. Once you identify the most important obstacle, you can involve the executives and skillfully manage their actions so that they «independently» identify this problem.

If you help them to identify this obstacle on their own, you'll see that later on it will be much easier to ensure that strategic plans are implemented. People like to be creative — make use of it!

The result of this phase is an exact wording of the identified obstacle or obstacles that are a priority for the company to overcome. In the next steps of the strategic planning cycle, you will need to monitor the planning process carefully to ensure your executives don't get sidetracked from solving the problem, and are targeted directly at it. This phase may take several days.

Discussing the problem with friends who are also business owners may be of great help to you in this process, as they will also have an outside viewpoint of your company's operations. Think carefully about who is worth talking to about it and who is not. It's very important that the person is positive and not inclined to criticism and to the devaluing of your ideas. If you choose the wrong person, the conversation could dissuade you from having anything to do with strategic planning, so be careful. If after a conversation with your friend, you feel like your interest in the growth of your company has lessened, don't talk to that person about the subject again. To snap out of the negative mood such a conversation can put you in, just dream about the wonderful future of your company.

Now you're ready for the third step: forming the main idea of your plan or plans. For example, this could be to get a loan from a bank, or to get raw materials from suppliers on credit (they too have an off-season and selling problems). At this step, you should involve the company executives and begin brainstorming.

Brainstorming is quite simple. Get all of the executives together in a separate room (never do it in their offices, as there are too many things there to distract them and remind them of routine problems). Let them know in advance that you'll need one to two hours of their time. Allow them to plan so that any current issues won't interrupt them. If this is impossible at the office, you could meet somewhere off-site. Just make sure that alcohol is excluded from the event, because alcohol doesn't contribute to creative thinking at all. Before beginning to brainstorm, report on the company's current situation and explain the problem for which they need to find a solution. Then explain to them these three rules of brainstorming:

1. Voice as many ideas as possible without any limits on creativity. These can be any ideas, even those that may at first seem unusual or strange.
2. Judging or devaluing of ideas is forbidden.
3. The brainstorming session must be organized.

The first rule is necessary because the more ideas a person

expresses, the more good ideas come to his mind. It's amazing. You may have noticed that while goofing around with friends and voicing various ideas, the ideas become more and more creative, sometimes to the surprise of their creators. The speed with which these ideas are expressed also matters. The faster the speed, the more the good ideas will come to you. You can easily encourage people to express more ideas by giving them a toothpick for each idea. At the end of the brainstorming session, the person with the most toothpicks is rewarded with a small prize or given a title like «Most Creative Employee.» People enjoy these kinds of games.

The second rule is important because a negative evaluation of any idea stops creativity. The idea of «healthy criticism» is all right for an assembly line, where it's necessary to sort out subquality work on the conveyor belt, but it is completely out of place in the area of creativity. Tell a person that now isn't the right time to implement the ideas she has suggested, that there is no money for their implementation, or that they are impractical for any reason, and she will run out of ideas. That's why when I hold brainstorming sessions, I make an agreement with the participants that any person who judges or devalues any idea takes everyone out for dinner. It works surprisingly well. Even people with lots of money don't like taking friends out to dinner as a penalty.

The third rule is that you need to manage this process. After you explain what the problem is, give those involved time to ask questions for clarification and try to answer these questions as accurately as possible. If they have ideas immediately, have them write them down. They shouldn't voice their ideas until everyone's questions on clarification have been answered. After this has been accomplished, let them think for a few moments—but not for too long. It doesn't take much time at all to come up with ideas. Usually people need time to get used to an idea they have come up with, or to seek some sort of confirmation, but this isn't necessary when brainstorming. Explain that anyone who wants to speak should raise his hand and that then you'll let him voice his idea. If participants interrupt one an other, it should be considered as devaluing the idea. Let them speak one at a time. Make them express their ideas quickly. Be sure to acknowledge every idea, but don't judge. Make it into a game. If you succeed at that, you will see enthusiasm and excitement and hear a number of excellent ideas. Be sure to arrange it so that someone briefly notes down every idea and its author.

The purpose of a brainstorming session is to generate lots of ideas without assessing their feasibility. After the brainstorming session is over, thank everyone who has expressed an idea. Then you can give your opinion on which idea you think was the best and why. Don't judge other ideas, not even to compare some of the ideas and discuss the advantages of some over others. You see, during a brainstorming session, you aren't acting as the owner. One of the responsibilities of an owner is to evaluate the performance of one's subordinates, but here, even owners aren't supposed to judge ideas—only evaluate results. The primary thing you want to gain from this step is the main idea (or ideas) for the strategic plan (or plans.) For example, one idea might be to pressure suppliers so that during the off-season they provide the necessary raw materials on credit, to be paid for at the beginning of the season. Other costs during this slow period will be paid for by using a bank line of credit. This will ensure a stable production level year-round by manufacturing the best-selling products during the off-season and storing them in a warehouse.

It is safe to say that the first three steps of the strategic management cycle completely determine the success of your strategy. The effectiveness of your strategy depends solely on how accurately you identify the problem.

I once consulted with the owner of a vinyl window–manufacturing company. His company was one of a number of these manufacturers operating in a city of over one million residents. He told me that his company manufactured and installed windows within about seven days, but that newer competitors could do it in just four. To increase sales, he'd decided to purchase new equipment for manufacturing the glass part of the window, which would reduce the production time of the window units. I asked him about the local market and found that his company had approximately a 3 percent share. Competitors who installed windows within four days had another 3 percent. The other 94 percent of the market was occupied by companies that produced and installed windows in seven or more days! It was obvious that by reducing manufacturing time, he would gain some advantage, but it was also obvious that this wasn't the biggest obstacle to his company's growth. When I asked him for information on the key performance indicators of the company's operations over the last five years, I found that two years earlier the company had stopped growing and had begun a gradual decline. When I asked what had changed in the company's operations two years earlier, I discovered that at that time the owner had fired a sales director, who, the owner claimed, had a dominating personality and ruined the lives of others. Surprisingly, after this «monster» was dismissed, revenues had stopped growing and the company had begun its decline. The owner, who had not been able to find a replacement this sales director, began managing the sales department himself. As I knew the owner pretty well by then, it was clear to me that he was an operations person to the roots of his hair and that sales was not his strength. So the marketing and sales area of the company had not been properly managed for two years, but the owner was trying to solve the company's growth problems through improvement of its production process. Instead of finding someone more suitable to manage the sales department, he preferred to buy new equipment. It was absolutely obvious that he did not like advertising and sales, did not like to sell, and greatly preferred to deal with the technical side of his business. I decided to calculate what not having a sale manager was costing him, and I arrived at a conservative estimate of more than forty thousand dollars per month. As soon as he heard this, he immediately came up with ideas on how to fix the situation. You see, by refusing to look at the real issue, he had been willing to spend money on the purchase of new equipment, which would not have produced significant results. It is important, therefore, to realise that the fruitfulness of your efforts to implement a strategy will depend on how well you perform the second step of the strategic management cycle: identifying the greatest obstacle to the company's growth.

After forming the main idea of the plan or plans, the fourth step is write up the strategic plans themselves. Let the executives do this. Don't give them too much time to do it; if you give them a week, they will write them up at the last minute anyway. Give them no more than about three to four hours. A strategic plan is quite free-form, but it should cover all possible questions. It's not a sequence of steps, but a description of the general sequence of actions: where to get funding for the implementation of the plan, who will be involved and what they will do, how to overcome the main obstacles to the plan's implementation, and what the desired results are. The strategic plans should contain a list of projects — to be written by the executives — that will lead to the successful implementation of the plan. And the strategic plan should have a well-defined goal.

A well-defined goal is an integral part of a strategic plan because it is impossible to try to implement something if you don't know exactly what you're striving for. On the other hand, it doesn't make any sense to set a goal if you have no idea how to achieve it. An approach such as «The most important thing is to set a goal and believe in it and there will be a way to reach it» doesn't work in company management. Every strategic plan has it's corresponding measurable, time-bound, and specific goal. It's important here not to confuse this goal with the main goal and purpose of the company.

For a good plan, one to two pages of text is usually enough. The most important thing is that if any executive reads the plan, he or she should have a pretty clear idea of what should be done and how to do it. For example, the strategic plan for the company manufacturing polypropylene thermal insulation could look like the following:

Strategic Plan for How to Increase Income

Our company has been losing a lot of money due to fluctuations of production volumes during the calendar year. We are forced to stay idle during the period from November to February, and then during the season we cannot handle all of the orders that come in. As a result, we lose qualified employees, sustain losses during the winter, and at the beginning of the season lose revenues because we are forced to turn away customers, who then go to our competitors. In order to fix these issues once and for all, we need to work during the off-season to produce our best-selling products and store them in a warehouse until the season starts. We need to gather information to determine the annual volume of standard products that can be produced to and the stored for subsequent sale, and calculate their manufacturing costs, including all production and salary expenses. Then we need to get prior approval for a bank line of credit. At the end of the season, we need to negotiate with our polypropylene suppliers to get raw materials on credit, with payment to be made at the beginning of the next season. There should be uninterrupted production during the entire year. The Human Resources Department should notify staff about changes to the vacation schedule in advance, since we will no longer have winter vacations! We also need to find a low-cost but reliable warehouse for storing our products, and an insurance company to insure our products while they are in the warehouse. Before the season begins, the Advertising Department should publish promotional materials that will inform our customers that they don't have to order products in advance, as they will be able to get them immediately from our warehouse.

In order to accomplish this plan, the following projects should be drawn up:

- Working capital mobilization project. The CFO (chief financial officer) is responsible for this. This project should include all the necessary calculations of production volumes.
- Staffing project. The director of Human Resources is responsible for this.
- Warehouse acquisition project. The COO (chief operations officer) is responsible for this.
- Advertising and sales project. The director of sales is responsible

for this.

The plan should be fully implemented by November 1 of this year. By that time, we should be fully staffed and ready for the planned workload.

Once we implement this plan, our company will reach a new level of growth and our operations will become easier and more efficient!

J. Smith
Owner

As each of your executives writes up his or her plans, you should review them, making sure that he or she didn't miss any points. And do you know what the best part is? At that moment, you will already get to see how well your executives will be able to carry out these plans. If in your review you see that the written plan is not feasible even on paper, then it certainly isn't going to happen in real life. If you encounter this, go over with the executive what wasn't understood about the main idea of the plan, and then have him continue so that a doable plan is made. Of course, you are likely to be tempted to rewrite it yourself. But then you'll have to bear the responsibility for the implementation of the plan, and your executive won't show much enthusiasm for its execution. If you take over the writing of the plan, you will create more problems for yourself. It's better to take the time to explain the ideas to the executives in question. You see, capable people don't like to be treated like robots and given precise, step-by-step instructions. Give the executive the opportunity to write the plans himself, and you'll see much more enthusiasm about their execution. Of course, if you are the owner, an executive, and directly manage key departments, then you will have to write some of the projects yourself. In this case, it's quite possible that the biggest obstacle to the growth of the company is the lack of executives, and you'll need to come up with some genius plan to solve this problem. Not sure if this problem has a solution? Just calculate how much it is costing you.

You've approved the strategic plans that contain lists of projects. The next step is to have the company executives appoint people to work on each project. Projects are lists of tasks. Each task has a particular date to be completed, and a person responsible for it.

I want to share my successful experience of how to make sure projects get written up quickly, even when you do it for the first time. As soon as you've approved the plans written by your top executives, organize a session on how to write projects. Get together everyone who wrote a plan, plus the people responsible for writing up the projects. Also invite your in-house experts and organize task forces to write the projects. For example, in the above example, one of the projects involved advertising and sales. Let the task force for this project consist of the best salesperson, the marketing manager, and the director of sales. Organize this session outside of regular business hours so that participants aren't distracted by routine affairs, and allocate four to six hours for this. Experience shows that if the session is held on a Saturday, executives apply themselves more diligently and try to finish more quickly.

At the beginning of the session, the authors of the strategic plans talk about their ideas in detail and answer questions from those responsible for writing the corresponding projects for the plans. For each project, its goal and how it relates to other projects is explained. Then the employees who are responsible for writing the projects begin drafting them, asking for additional clarification from the authors of the plans as needed. Once the projects have been written, each author presents his and describes its sequence of tasks, and then the executives can make their corrections. Within a few hours, you can have good projects written, the execution of which will lead to the implementation of the strategic plans.

Before the tasks listed on the projects are started, the owner needs to approve them, making sure they correspond to the strategic plans. Also, he or she must assess whether they really solve the problem that was identified in the second step of strategic planning. Once the projects receive the owner's approval, they become mandatory.

In my experience, the two most common mistakes made in the strategic planning cycle are:

- The main obstacle or obstacles that the strategic plans are targeted to address have been incorrectly identified.
- There is no systematic control over the execution of the tasks of the projects.

The first of these mistakes has already been discussed, but it should be noted that in medium- and large-size companies this mistake has a different characteristic. In these companies, the second step (identifying the biggest obstacle to growth) is performed by top executives who, instead of identifying the main problem, identify dozens of less significant problems, then make plans to solve these issues. As a result, the company's strategy resembles chaos—no priorities but lots of activity. Even with good oversight of the execution of the tasks of projects, in this situation the company's resources are used inefficiently. With the correct approach, the company can achieve much better results.

One error that is commonly made by untrained personnel is to jump from purpose to tactical planning, omitting the strategic plan.

The point to be understood here is that strategic planning creates tactical planning. One won't get one's purpose achieved unless there is a strategy worked out and used by which to achieve it[23].

The chairman of the board of directors of a large insurance company asked me to evaluate how well strategic planning was implemented at his company. The company had a special strategy adviser, whom I questioned regarding how the company's strategic planning was performed, and I obtained the strategic plans for the current year from him. I found that they began the strategic planning cycle at the second-to-last step, where a manager from each department writes down a list of strategic tasks for his or her department. Then they merely combined these tasks into one general list. It was impossible to understand what the strategy was, for the simple reason that there was no strategy—just a pile of tasks targeted toward the improvement of particular departments. After they did this each year, the execution of the tasks for the «strategic activities» (as they called them) was unmanageable. Even if someone tried to control the process, it would simply be impossible.

It is quite common in tactical execution of a strategic plan to find it necessary to modify some tactical targets or add new ones or even drop out some as found to be unnecessary[24].

As soon as you approve the projects, begin to oversee their execution, and require your executives to complete their tasks in a timely manner, you will discover that your strategy is not perfect. You will find that you aren't at the very top of the «Tone Scale of Decisions.» Your plans will contain particular points that are impossible to execute, and some important issues concerning associated projects will not have been taken into account. This is absolutely normal. If you get a weekly report from executives on the progress of each approved project, you will be able to find out quickly what things were planned incorrectly and thus can fix them. If you don't oversee the execution of the projects, the projects and their corresponding strategic plans will quietly and unwittingly die, and this is very bad. First, the company will not grow. Second, executives begin to feel that plan or no plan, nothing good comes out of them anyway, and the idea of strategic planning itself will lose value. Then the next time you enthusiastically begin to create or breathe life back into your plan, you won't start

---

[23] L. Ron Hubbard, «Strategic Planning,» in The Management Series, vol. 1 (Los Angeles: Bridge Publications, 2001), 286.

[24] L. Ron Hubbard, «Strategic Planning,» in The Management Series, vol. 1 (Los Angeles: Bridge Publications, 2001), 285.

from zero, but from a negative position. Negative experiences, as a rule, do not empower people.

An interesting fact is that the majority of companies are just graveyards of incomplete projects. They're full of the wreckage of great ideas that were never completely brought to life. When I consult for such companies, I recommend rehabilitating this wreckage before introducing new plans. To accomplish this, a list is made of all of the projects that were started and never completed. Then it is decided whether each project will become a part of the new plans or will be rejected entirely. Of course, you should let your executives know about your plans for these old projects before adding more to their plates.

I hope that everything I've written about strategic management will not seem too complicated to you. I want to assure you that a number of companies of various sizes, even small ones consisting of only a few employees, have successfully used this tool and grown rapidly as a result. You don't want to spend the next fifty years creating a successful company, do you? Then don't delay. Begin the cycle of strategic management in your company.

Chapter 13

....

Finances and Assets

In the area of financial management, most business owners cannot escape a vicious cycle: The company's executives do not take responsibility for the financial performance of the company. Therefore, the company owner alone makes all major financial decisions. As she holds all financial matters in her hands, no one else is responsible for them. When the time comes to pay wages, she is only one concerned with whether the company has enough funds to make payroll, or whether the revenues of the company are high enough to cover salaries and other expenses. Certainly, the amount of money that a company makes doesn't address this fundamental issue, as you know very well that people are talented money exterminators. No matter how much money is made, they can always spend more. The same applies to company assets, which are materialized money.

In order to understand how to break out of this cycle, let's look at a very important principle described by L. Ron Hubbard in one of his articles[25]. It's a law called the «Triangle of Knowledge-Responsibility-Control,» and also the «Triangle of Competency.» The main idea of this law is that a person proportionally builds his or her knowledge, responsibility, and ability to control. For example, it is impossible to increase responsibility to a high level if a person does not have knowledge and the ability to control.

Here the word *knowledge* refers to possessing some information or having familiarity with a particular field of activity. You can tell whether a person knows the rules of the road if she can precisely specify, without hesitation, how to act in a given situation.

The word *control* in the context means «guidance; management.» That is, control is the ability to direct an activity, put it in motion in the right direction, start the motion, revise the direction of the movement, and stop it. A skilled tennis player has good control over the ball. She can change the speed and direction of its flight and return it in the desired direction. A good driver controls his car. He has complete

[25] L. Ron Hubbard, «The Top Triangle,» in The Management Series, vol. I, (Los Angeles: Bridge Publications, Inc., 2001), 377.

control of its movements, and when he cannot handle its operation, we say that he has «lost control.» A good dancer exercises great bodily control. If you ask women, many will tell you that they enjoy it when they are led (controlled) while dancing.

Responsibility refers to an acknowledgment of oneself as the cause of something happening. It includes the ability to make decisions and act. Responsibility, in its essence, is a person's decision regarding whether he is the cause of some action or consequence. Having gotten into a car accident, a person can either acknowledge himself as the cause of the accident or he can claim that someone else was the cause. Responsibility is often confused with guilt, but guilt is a completely different concept. Guilt is when a person considers himself to be the cause of something bad. It can be said that the awareness of guilt is the acknowledgment of responsibility for consequences that a person considers to be negative. When a person does not acknowledge himself as the reason for something that happened in his life, he is refusing to manage that area of his life. If a husband says that his wife is a witch, that she is spoiled, and it is her fault that his life is so miserable, then he has completely refused to manage his relationship with her. If he acknowledges personal responsibility for his own choices, he at least has the choice to divorce her. A person's level of responsibility predetermines his ability to act. If there is no responsibility, there is no action. For example, a company owner complains that the motivation of the people who come to work for her company is no good. She says that all they're interested in is getting money at any cost, and that because of this attitude, they're ruining her business. She claims that money is the only reason people are willing to work, and that she is unable to motivate them. If she has made such a decision, things would look bleak, as she wouldn't even try to change the situation.

The three vertices of the triangle, Knowledge-Responsibility-Control (KRC), are interrelated. When a person grows along the knowledge dimension of the triangle, for example, by learning about how leaders can influence the motivation of staff, she begins to attempt to control the area. She begins to advance goals and purposes and inspire employees. Thus, she also progresses along the control dimension, as she can create and direct actions. By exercising control, she gets some results: Some of the staff begin to show more enthusiasm at work, while others fiercely rejects the leader's ideas. Having faced her role in obtaining these results and realizing the consequences of her control, the leader recognizes that she is the cause of these results. It's easy and enjoyable if the results are positive; it is more difficult if the consequences of control are destructive.

You could say that the rate at which someone progresses along the responsibility dimension of the triangle depends on how much courage that person has to see the consequences for what they really are. If the consequences of his actions are so bad that he cannot bear to look at them and acknowledge personal responsibility for what has happened, this leads to a degradation of the person, and his KRC in this area is diminished. An example of this would be a person who is involved in a serious car accident as a result of losing control of his car and then refuses to ever drive again. This is an ostrich's favorite tactic — hiding its head in the sand.

If you want to raise your child to be able to manage money, you must first give him some knowledge about money. You explain what money is, where it comes from, and what role it plays in life. Then you give him the opportunity to make money, and to spend it. He gets control of money. He uses it and learns some lessons. He learns about the ability to buy something he wants, and the inability to buy something he wants when he doesn't have enough money. If you help your child realize the consequence of his actions, he'll have a more responsible attitude toward money. He'll seek to learn more about it and how to control it better. Of course, as a caring parent, you won't give him the opportunity to skin his knees too much when it comes to handling money. I want to mention that part of learning about the control of money should always include the opportunity to make money. Many of my friends created opportunities for their children to earn money by paying them to do certain chores and helping them out. The children of wealthy parents who have never had control over making money and spending it don't acquire the responsibility to provide for themselves and, unfortunately, often grow dependent.

This principle of cultivating a sense of responsibility also works beautifully in a company. If you want executives to acknowledge themselves as the reason for the profits and losses of the company, you need to cultivate an awareness of this responsibility in accordance with KRC. This means that first they must have an understanding of the company's finances. You will never be able to create competency in a person if he has no knowledge. This means that executives should have accurate and current information about all revenues and expenditures of the company, should know the sources and amounts of these revenues, as well as the level of expenses for the company. From this viewpoint, you can see that concealing the financial situation of the company from its executives while trying to get them to exhibit a responsible attitude seems a ridiculous practice. A policy of confidentiality regarding information on revenues and expenses will always lead to irresponsibility. I'm not suggesting that every employee should have access to this information, but it should be available to the company's top executives. Moreover, the information about the company's income is almost impossible to hide, and very often executives will have the false idea that the company is making a lot of money, simply because they have no idea about the level and structure of its expenditures.

The second component in cultivating this sense of responsibility among your executives is providing them with control over revenues and expenditures. Currently you provide them with the opportunity to control revenues when you create targets for sales, but do you provide them with the same degree of control over expenses? Ideally, they should be able to fully utilize all of the revenues of the company within the rules established by you as the owner. These rules should describe how to handle working capital[26] and reserves, how much should be distributed to shareholders, and how much can be spent on salaries and other expenses. Establishment of these rules and oversight of their application is a part of the owner's function. Control is exercised through departmental budgeting and regular meetings on the allocation of funds.

There is a «useful» budgeting technique that often results in a lack of control for the company's executives. Here executives help to create a budget for a longer period, such as a year or a quarter, but then all of the day-to-day decisions regarding allocation of funds are made by either the chief financial officer or the Owner. In this case, one person is actually in control and the other executives are «out of work» so to speak, as they are no longer involved in the company's financial decisions, and they are not truly able to do their jobs without this ability. That is why the only correct approach is to organize budgeting in such a way that executives can really make decisions on how funds are allocated, and higher-level authorities (that is, the CEO or CFO) just monitor these allocations to ensure they are reasonable and in line with established policies.

The third component is that the sense of responsibility increases when executives are able to observe the consequences of their actions with respect to the allocation of funds. A couple of weeks ago, they allocated money for advertising. What were the results? They updated computer equipment, or bought a new machine. How did it effect the company's performance? If a company has a precise system of performance assessment for all of its divisions, it will be possible to

---

[26] Working capital is the capital that is used in the day-to-day operations of company, calculated as the current assets minus the current liabilities.

measure accurately the results of particular expenditures. Then when the weekly allocation of funds is made, executives will be able to make wiser decisions. If they know it was their decision to allocate money for the purchase of new equipment, then they will feel they are the reason why the new equipment made the company stronger, or proved to be useless. This is how a sense of responsibility is cultivated.

Don't think the executives will necessarily set about this work with enthusiasm. In 2003, when I organized meetings with our executives to allocate funds for the first time, they completely refused to do so on the grounds that «it wasn't necessary.» They «trusted me» as the owner, so «why change anything?» By the way, «We trust you» often means «We don't want to take any responsibility for it; let someone else take the responsibility.» This is why I had to insist and say, «Guys, we now have new rules. It will never be like it used to be again. Here are the guidelines by which you will allocate all of the money received by the company. Get to work; as divisional executives, this is your new responsibility!» Of course, everything didn't go smoothly. I broke a sweat a few times while teaching them how to hold fund-allocation meetings quickly and accurately, but I can't say it was too difficult. What really pleased me after a while were the incredible changes in their viewpoints about the production level of the company. For a long time, I'd been trying to put forth the idea that we needed to increase production levels in order for the company to grow. My operations manager constantly grumbled that our production facility couldn't produce more than sixty to eighty thousand units a week because we had poor equipment and insufficient space. After the new principles regarding fund allocations were introduced and he'd gained some experience with them, he said, «If we buy some tools and hire a few more people, we can produce one hundred twenty thousand units per week.» Three months later he claimed that with the same space we could produce up to 180,000 per week. This was an amazing transformation in his point of view. In three months, I saw that all of the executives who participated in funds allocation had changed their viewpoints on the revenues and expenses of the company. I never had to worry about setting aside reserves again, they were so good at allocating money. I would never be able to do it as well. The fact is, there is always some disagreement when it comes to the allocation of money, as there are many needs, and the amount of money the company has is limited. Accordingly, executives have to prove to one an other the reasonableness for and the return on certain expenditures.

Since 2003, as the owner of multiple companies, I have not directly handled the allocation of funds, but have only supervised the process.

For me, this management tool, first and foremost, is one of the resources that allows you to raise the responsibility level of your executives to ensure that they consider the successes and failures of the company as their own.

There is another interesting law regarding money: «The income potential of any usual group is established by the demand for income, not by any other important factor.»[27] The amount of revenue made is determined not by what an organization considers to be desirable to have, but by what it must have. In other words, the revenues of an organization and of an individual depend on the levels of need.

I used to have a friend who was a broker, a middleman. He ordered products from our company and supplied them to various government departments and agencies. He could do this thanks to his ability to make and maintain connections. Since I knew his sales volume and selling prices, I was aware of how much money he made. It was quite a lot of money. I'd always been amazed at how modest he appeared, including the type of car he drove. He had a Subaru that was probably more than twenty years old — at least that's how it looked. In spite of his high income, he was always modest in his spending. This lasted for about three years. One day I arrived at my office and saw a brand-new Citroën in the parking lot, clearly just from the dealership. It was so unusual for him to have made such a purchase, I couldn't resist asking what had happened in his life. He told me how a few years earlier he had worked as a state employee in one of the government ministries, and how one of his relatives had proposed that they jointly start what promised to be an incredibly profitable business. In order to start it, they needed money, which my friend borrowed from one of his wealthy friends. The business failed, but the debt remained. The size of the debt had been such that even over a lifetime he would not have been able to pay it off on his state employee's salary. That was why he started his brokering business. At the end of the story, he added, «If it hadn't been for that debt and the need to repay that money, I would never have learned to make so much money.»

I think you'll agree with this concept if you consider your own experience. If you are accustomed to a certain level of expenditures, it's practically impossible to lower them. Instead, you need to increase your level of income. When company executives first begin allocating funds for the company and encounter a situation where there is not enough money, their first instinct is to cut expenses.

---

[27] L. Ron Hubbard, «Building Fund Account,» in The Management Series, vol. 3, (Los Angeles: Bridge Publications, 2001), 398.

As a consultant, I usually give them some time to play around with this idea. As a rule, it takes them only a couple of hours spent in meetings to realize that it is practically impossible to cut expenses without harming production. When they grow tired of this game, I suggest they look at the main principle that should be used when allocating money: The allocation of funds by the Finance Department for the operations of a company or a particular part of a company must be for buying something. At this point, really good ideas come to their minds. This method works especially well when strategic planning is well established in the company and its level of expenses is determined not only by how much it needs to survive comfortably right now but also by how much it needs in order to implement its strategic plans. Sometimes you have to handle frustrations, and even tears, when the head of a department realizes for the first time what the financial situation is. It's like looking into the abyss. The first time, it is unbearably terrifying. The second time, it's easier. After some time, one begins to see what is at the bottom of the abyss. Different people have different levels of preparedness when it comes to managing money. Therefore the training of managers in money management needs to be gradual, and there need to be rules and oversight of the training process.

When you formulate the rules for allocating funds by which the executives will be guided, it's important not to create a condition of micromanagement. The rules should not deprive the executives of control by describing every breath they take. I witnessed a situation where executives had gathered for a fund-allocation meeting. The finance director read out information about how the money was to be allocated in accordance with the rules. Everybody obediently nodded their heads, then left wondering, Why did we need to have this meeting? Control entails some freedom of action. At our Business Owners Program — a consulting project delivered to clients by our consulting company — we discuss how to implement financial planning and conduct meetings with the executives. During these discussions, I'm often asked whether an executive should be allowed to defer a bill payment in order to pay wages, and why, if the fee for a late bill payment is not too high, should they not actually defer the bill payment. A meeting of executives includes the chief accountant. If he agrees with the decision to defer payment, then why not spend the money on something useful to the company? I don't see any issues here. If funds are allocated weekly and there are controls over it, executives cannot make catastrophic mistakes. Small failures will just push them to act more effectively. They will learn from their experiences and become more responsible. It's impossible to make a person responsible if you completely protect him from all possible mistakes.

One more important function of the business owner is to control the valuable assets of the company. It often happens that when an owner starts a company, he provides office space and equipment. However, as soon as operations begin, the beautifully renovated office, the office equipment, and the manufacturing machines start to depreciate with every passing week. Sometimes it even reaches an extreme where an owner ends up with a yearly profit from the company of one million dollars, but the company's assets (equipment and property) depreciate during this same period by two million dollars. The owner, in fact, has become poorer by a million dollars, but he'll only feel it when the equipment falls into disrepair and stops working. To avoid this, it is important for the accounting department to accurately take stock of all tangible and intangible assets, continuously calculate their depreciation, and reflect this in its reports. Then it becomes possible to accurately assess what happens to a company's assets. Executives can then be required to make up for the depreciation of assets by finding ways for the company to earn additional, offsetting revenue, or (which often happens as a rule in growing companies) purchase new assets that are higher in value than the depreciation of current assets.

Money, by its nature, is energy. And how skillfully a company manages this energy will determine the success and speed of its growth. But the management of this energy is a routine function and is not the job of the owner. But as the owner, you will need to do some work to organize the financial management of the company properly.

Chapter 14

....

The Duties of the Business Owner

In the previous chapters, I have discussed the most important functions of a business owner. Now I will summarize this information.

Every company has an owner, and a goal. The owner of company has a specific responsibilities and a specific goal. The owner's goal can be stated as follows: Unite, inspire, and guide talented people toward making an outstanding product.

Of course, for a period of time every founder of a business performs other tasks in his company: selling, managing personnel, handling finances, and so forth. But while he is able to perform tasks other than those of the owner, there is no one who is able to perform his tasks. An owner can work as a salesperson, but a salesperson cannot perform the tasks of the owner. When Visotsky Consulting helps an owner organize his company's operations, our company frequently encounters a situation in which an owner has to choose between working on improving his company's operations or focusing on personally handling problems and growth the way he's been doing. In this case, I suggest looking at what each option leads to in the long run. If the company's operations are not streamlined, then the larger the company grows, the less effective its operations will become, and the more time they will take away from the owner. And the more the company grows, the more difficult it will be to streamline its operations. This process is similar to working by hand rather than using tools. In the beginning, the difference won't be as noticeable, but as operations scale up, the difference will have a much greater impact on results.

Of course, learning how to master even a simple tool takes time away from your work while you learn how to use it. If a person needs to type on a computer a lot and doesn't know how to touch-type, he'll waste a lot of time hunting for keys on the keyboard. I once calculated that if I continued typing like most people, using only two fingers, then with the amount of typing I do, I would spend over three years of my life hunting for the correct keys to press. It shocked me! That's why I spent about thirty hours learning how to type correctly. But three years is nothing compared to how much of an owner's time is eaten up by a company that is not properly organized. It will consume all of your time—and even that won't be enough. Don't believe me? Just conduct a stopwatch study[28] of your workday, then analyze what you were doing during that time.

When it came time to hire a CEO and relinquish the daily management of my company, I needed to write down all of my responsibilities. I thought I was a so-so CEO because I didn't like to deal with the discipline or routine coordination of employees. In order to create a job description for the future CEO, I started to conduct daily stopwatch studies of my working hours and noted what I did each day. At the end of each week, I analyzed the results and determined which duties I performed as CEO and which I performed as an owner. As a result, I wrote a pretty good description of the responsibilities of the CEO. But I realized that I'd done almost nothing as an owner. I found that all of my time was being consumed by the CEO job, and I was an owner only somewhere deep in my heart. At first, I thought it was amazing that I was able to create a relatively well-run enterprise at all. Then I realized the results could have been several times better if I had met my responsibilities as an owner first and foremost.

Every job position has its own product. Here, by *product*, we mean the end result of one's activities in a particular job. Each job has its own specific product; job duties are performed, and the job itself exists for the purpose of creating this product. A salesperson's work ultimately yields signed contracts and revenues. An accountant provides spotless records and reports. A janitor has to maintain a facility's cleanliness and keep things in proper working order. The owner's position also has specific product. Because he is at the top of the management hierarchy, he is responsible for everything that happens on the levels below his. For example, the director of sales' product is sales for the entire department, as well as the sales made by each salesman. The product the business owner should produce can be stated as: «a successful, growing company with a stable financial position.»

Successful here means the company achieves its purpose in spite of any obstacles. Regarding growth, I sometimes come across a pretty strange point of view—namely, that every business has reasonable limits beyond which it should not go. Yes, if you own a restaurant, then sooner or later you will almost always reach a ceiling and limits related to its location that will prevent further expansion. But there is always the opportunity to open another restaurant. The only limit that can really arise is if you, while implementing the purpose, become a

---

[28] A stopwatch study involves studying and recording the duration of time various processes and particular procedures require.

monopolist. Then you really wouldn't be able to grow further without expansion of the purpose of your company. I personally haven't faced such a problem yet. It makes sense to grow any business. «Reasonable limits» is just an excuse, behind which is always the inability to solve some problem. Let's return to the wording of the product of the owner's position. «A stable financial position» is a condition in which a company is able to weather any crisis, and this can be achieved by having safely allocated cash reserves and maintaining a good balance of revenues and expenses.

Regarding products, there is an interesting idea: If a person cannot name his product, then he is not able to make it happen. Because I tend to question things, I decided to verify this. In conversations with executives, I asked them questions to determine what they considered to be the product of their position. I was shocked by the results. The most productive executives could pretty clearly name their products; the most unproductive ones came up with some really absurd things. The director of operations believed that his product was ensuring the efficiency of operations of the production process (but not the products that were produced). Another executive even told me that his product was the support his supervisor (that is, his *help* was his product). That was like a blow to my head.

Naturally, if there is a product, there is always a way to measure how its quantity changes over time, and to know how successfully the person responsible for it is in producing it. The owner's product can also be measured. Actually, you measure it every time you say that your company has increased its revenues or profits by a certain percentage compared with the previous year. But it's important not to make this mistake in your evaluation: If your company's income has grown by only a few percent, this is not really growth—it is merely running in place. There is inflation and the increase of other business expenses each year. We can say that in business it is impossible to maintain a stable state; there is always either significant growth or a contraction. If a small company has grown in a year by only 10 percent, it is breathing, but not very well. For a small company, it is normal to have at least 30 percent growth each year, but even that rate cannot be considered good.

In previous chapters, I have discussed most of the functions a business owner performs to produce his or her product. Here they are again:

- Formation of the company's main goal and purpose and their preservation and promotion to form the ideological basis for the company's operations

- Creation and development of the company's product in accordance with changing market conditions and technology changes
- Establishment and approval of policies that define the rules to facilitate the achievement of the company's purpose
- Establishment and improvement of the company's technology
- Organization of strategic planning and the strategic management cycle for controllable growth and the achievement of intermediate goals
- Organization of rational and effective management of money and material assets
- Establishment and training of the top executives in their positions and oversight of their activities (there will be a separate book on this subject)

I don't know whether the volume of these responsibilities struck terror in you while reading the previous chapters, but to a certain extent you are already performing these functions. Your company is tangible proof of that. Imagine what your company would be today if you had devoted significantly more time to these particular owner's functions.

What should you do if you find yourself in a position in which you have to take on the roles of a business owner and CEO simultaneously? I have personally experienced this situation. In the morning, while driving to work, you think about which important improvements to execute in the company and which new plans to implement. But at the end of the day, you pry yourself away from your desk and can't remember what you were doing all day.

In order to do important work, two components are necessary. They are time and space. It is impossible to create a successful strategy for a company «on the fly» while hundreds of various matters distract your attention. Even in our consulting projects, we will occasionally pull an owner out of his environment in order to work on policy documents with him. If you really want to perform the functions of an owner, you need to make sure you have time and space sufficient to allow you to work on the most important matters without being distracted. You need time and a place that you can regularly devote to this work without any distractions, because work that is constantly interrupted takes much longer to complete, and very often doesn't get completed at all. Let's look at the actions you need to take to successfully perform the functions listed above.

Formation of the Company's Main Goal and Purpose

At a minimum the main goal and purpose of the company should be established, defined in a policy, and understood by every employee. It is important to mention the main goal and purpose of the company during every general staff meeting and in meetings with the executives. Occasionally, you will refine them.

Creation and Improvement of the Product

You need to attend exhibitions, read trade magazines, and gather information on what your competitors are doing. It's also good practice to study the experiences of more advanced companies in the same industry, as this can provide you with a good idea of the future of the industry. It's important to keep up with changes in production technology, business law issues, and ways to promote products. Technology companies need to develop and benefit from these changes. You need to create, approve, and oversee the plans regarding the improvement of your company's product.

Creation and Approval of Policies

You must constantly monitor the activities of the company, identify deviations from desired performance, establish policies to address these points, and ensure that employees are aware of the policies and follow them.

Establishment and Improvement of the Company's Technology

You must find people who are able to define your company's technology in the form of company policies. You should study closely the successful technologies that already exist by reading books, attending seminars, and looking for talented experts whom you can invite to join your company.

One of our clients has a successful practice. He searches the country for talented experts who have valuable knowledge and invites them to work for his company for a year. He comes to an exact agreement with them on what the results of their work should be, provides them with housing and a salary, and, upon achievement of the intended results, he pays them a good bonus. It may seem like an expensive approach, but just think about what it really costs your company to learn how to make its product. How much money would you have saved if you had learned how to do this within a year instead of five years?

Organization of Strategic Planning and Oversight of the Execution of Plans

This function requires weekly work. Not only is it necessary to spend a few days to launch a strategy, but it is also necessary to monitor the process of the project's execution on a weekly basis. Meetings with executives should be conducted in order to coordinate their actions and direct them toward the desirable result. Ever since I appointed a CEO and began to manage the company from the position of the owner, this function has taken at least four hours a week. Once every six months, it takes a few days to adjust plans and form new ones.

Organization of Proper Handling of Finances and Assets

The establishment of the proper handling of finances and assets takes a lot of time in the beginning, when everything needs to be organized. After that, it will take an hour a week to read and check reports, and to adjust anything if necessary.

Contrary to how it may sound, all of this doesn't add up to that much time. Performing all of these functions adds up to one working day per week. Note that I have not mentioned a single function of a CEO — only the functions of an owner. If you realize that the product of your position as owner is to «unite, inspire, and guide talented people toward making an outstanding product,» you will work more and more toward this goal and will see how quickly your company can grow. If you can achieve twofold annual growth for your company each year, you will be able to achieve within fifteen years what McDonald's achieved in fifty-eight years.

Today, companies can grow very rapidly because they have the support of modern means of communication, training, and automation. Forty years ago, it would have taken weeks to carry out a training program for employees who worked in nearby towns. Now it takes just a few hours. Previously, you would have needed months to introduce a new product, and now it can be done within a few days by using videos and the Internet. The modern business arena provides unprecedented opportunities for fast and effective growth. Only competent business owners will be able to take full advantage of this.

You might wonder how outstanding companies are able to grow and thrive even when their founders do not completely fulfill all of their functions as business owners. You would be right in concluding that not all business owners fulfill all of their functions. The business world is not so cruel, and it forgives a number of mistakes. In order to thrive, it is important not to make the worst ones. If McDonald's had grown at least 25 percent annually during the past fifty-eight years of its history, today there would be ten times as many McDonald's restaurants as there are now.

Chapter 15

....

Co-Owners and Power

In the year when the number of completed consulting projects for my company exceeded one hundred, I decided to gather statistics on the companies that had multiple owners. The results were the following: About 30 percent of the companies had multiple owners. In only 40 percent of these companies did the existence of multiple owners have a positive effect on the companies' operations. For the remainder, it was harmful to the businesses.

Don't think that co-owners in a company are always a problem, because that isn't the case. I have consulted with companies in which co-owners cooperated perfectly. More often, however, I've encountered companies in which the co-owners had actively cooperated during the first stages of the company's growth, but after a period of time conflicts emerged between them that developed into serious issues. There are a number of examples of such companies. McDonald's experienced such an issue. At the very beginning, Ray Kroc and the McDonald brothers successfully cooperated and grew the company. But after six years, the McDonald brothers, believing the company had not made enough profit, issued Kroc an ultimatum and demanded he buy out their rights to the trademark. In order to satisfy their demands, Kroc had to attract outside investments. Perhaps this was a kind of push for the company to grow. Steve Jobs was forced to leave Apple under pressure from the board of directors nine years after the beginning of successful operations. The majority of Ukrainian companies that have multiple owners usually experience a crisis after five to ten years of operation.

Sometimes the conflicts can be settled, but they can almost never be eliminated entirely. Why do talented, positive people initially cooperate but over time begin to have more and more differences with one another? I went through this with my own business partners, and only a few years ago did I realized why it had happened. There is a fundamental law that, if ignored, will doom partnerships to failure. This law is very simple: Supreme authority can belong to only one person. When we establish a partnership, we usually forget to discuss subjects such as who is in charge, who will establish the goals, and who can have the final say about what is right and what is not for the company.

What, then, are meetings of executives and democratic governing bodies for? In terms of management, any meeting is a tool in the hands of a superior and can be used to find solutions and coordinate the actions required for their execution. Meetings are productive only if someone is in charge of them. The person who has authority organizes the meetings, raises the questions that need to be addressed, and requires the execution of approved solutions.

At the heart of any corporation, there is always a particular contradiction. On the one hand, shareholders invest their money in the company because the person setting the goals for the company has demonstrated his competence. On the other, large shareholders begin to interfere with the operations of the company through the board of directors[29]. Often these interferences create devastating consequences. An example of this would be the period of when Steve Jobs was absent from Apple. During this time Apple's management tried to grow the company without adhering to the purpose and policies that had been the basis of its success. Blinded by its initial successes, Apple made a number of mistakes (Macintosh clones[30], the expansion of its product line, the transition to RISC-based PowerPC processors[31]). Frankly, ever since Jobs died, I have been closely watching to see whether the company would follow his principles, and I am disappointed with what is happening. Once the company lost its leader and goal setter, the company's management began to express its creativity. As such, Apple announced it would launch a new iPad in a smaller size in September 2012. The company wanted to make the tablet more affordable. My prediction is that in the long run, this is the beginning of the end for Apple. An attempt to reduce their products to the level of mass-produced goods and compete in the low-price segment will sooner or later destroy the brand. Creativity that ruins the purpose and policies of a company is a direct path to oblivion. The problem is that Jobs apparently never fully described the ideology of the company and

---

[29] A board of directors is a management body in a joint venture. Its members are elected at the shareholders' meeting. Any private individual, not necessarily a shareholder, can become a member of the board of directors. The purpose of the board of directors is to manage the operation of the company in the shareholders' best interest.

[30] Computers with the Apple operating system produced under license by other manufacturers (Motorola, Power Computing, UMAX).

[31] RISC-based PowerPC processor is a microprocessor based on the RISC platform, created in 1991 by the joint efforts of Apple, IBM, and Motorola, known as AIM. When Apple first began to use these processors, there were predictions that they were promising for use in personal computers. To this day, these predictions have not been justified.

did not establish clear-enough policies on the process of creating new products. That is why the result is pretty obvious: Their products will gradually degrade, which sooner or later will destroy the company.

No matter how many co-owners or shareholders are in a company, there must be one person who has the highest authority. She takes on the function of establishing goals and, naturally, has the final say in matters of dispute. This does not mean that she has to be a tyrant who imposes her will by force. Sometimes, however, it is necessary if this is the only way to achieve a result. But this approach doesn't work when managing people who are expected to express creativity at work. The person who has authority should understand that her main task is to unite creativity, grant power to her partners and authorized executives, and build consent with respect to the ideology of the company. Because Visotsky Consulting is actively expanding and today the distance between our offices is about five thousand miles, I have to manage people from a great distance. This is a new experience for me, because the greater the distance is, the better the mutual understanding needs to be. You see, when you have such distance between you and your employees, you cannot just send orders to them. You need to achieve significant agreement for your policies to work. I need to conduct a meeting of the board of directors weekly in order to reach such agreement, to inspire them to achieve, and to discuss with them the largest-scale problems, plans, and policies. Thankfully, Skype and Google have provided us with convenient tools, as before these technologies this would have been difficult to accomplish.

You have authority over people the moment they acknowledge your right to prioritize activities. The person who sets the goals possesses the highest authority. If there are multiple owners, they should understand this principle and agree that one of them sets the goals and the rest follow his ideas. If there is no agreement between them, then as soon as they begin to have different opinions on priorities regarding the growth of the company, the dissidence begins. In Kazakhstan, I was asked to settle a conflict between two co-owners of a trading company. One had 60 percent of the shares, and the other 40. The first was initially an investor and the second was the person who set the goals. The second co-owner had started this business and had been managing it for several years. The conflict started with the dissatisfaction of the 60 percent co-owner with the priorities regarding the growth of the company. The three of us talked for about two hours and they settled their differences. The only thing I did during that time was to clarify the functions of an owner of a company, and then help them to remember and restore their original agreement regarding the division of these functions. Of course, I made sure that this time the agreement was in writing and signed by both parties. Their original agreement was actually that one of them was empowered to set the goals, handle product and process development, and be responsible for strategic planning, while the other would invest money and handle finances and asset management. But years had passed since then, and since the clear agreement on their functions and responsibilities originally had not been written down, over time the co-owners' ideas on what the agreement was had transformed. Had they not returned to their initial agreement, they most likely would have begun to have serious problems with the business.

The transformation of people's ideas on a subject over time is a very natural thing. As time goes by, an individual experiences new things, gains knowledge, and begins to look at the environment around him differently. In fact, as he grows, it's guaranteed that in time he will have a different point of view about the company he works in and the state of affairs there. If you make sure that the agreement is solid and stated in writing, then even if one of the owners develops a different point of view, the agreement will have to be modified before he may begin to act differently.

The person who sets the goals should make sure that all co-owners take on certain functions of the owner. For example, one can handle the product and technology, while the other sets the goals and handles the ideology, policies, and strategy of the company. If every co-owner has personal and separate areas of responsibility, then the company is easy to manage, since it is possible to assess results and coordinate actions. In general, any collaboration begins with an understanding of who will perform what functions. It is impossible to cooperate if, first, there is no clear understanding of what the functions of each party are, and, second, there is no clear distinction between these functions. Concepts of *collaboration* and *coordination*, on their own, necessitate making distinctions about the functions of those who collaborate. The situation where everyone is responsible for everything, in reality, means that nobody is responsible for anything.

In addition, it sometimes happens that upon achieving a particular level of growth, a company begins to actively accumulate good partnership connections and sign long-term contracts that can significantly strengthen it. This happens when a company has already learned how to produce its product well. This becomes obvious even to other companies. In other words, the company begins to be recognized as one that performs a particular function. This is a result of internal cooperation. If partners cannot agree on what each one of them is responsible for, there is a situation of too many cooks spoiling the soup. An example of such a company is one in which there is no secretary and any available employee picks up the phone when it rings. In this case, it's almost impossible to make sure that the responses to phone calls follow established guidelines.

If you don't provide a co-owner with particular responsibilities, you will inevitably have troubles, as she will try to influence operations. Since she doesn't have a personal area of responsibility, she will invade yours. In management, there is a principle: Either you direct a person's creative energy toward goals or she will direct it toward something of her own choice, and you will have to deal with the consequences. Why are soldiers in an army forced to do a lot of busywork? Why will an experienced officer never leave his soldiers without work, even if he has to make something up for them to do? It is because if people are left alone and no one controls their actions, they will find something to do themselves. But soldiers have weapons. It's an primitive example, but it demonstrates this principle very well.

I recognized this concept of partners needing to have specific functions several years ago. Once I realized this, I signed agreements with the co-owners of each of the three companies I co-owned. The agreements clearly laid out the goals of our partnerships and each of our functions. It specified who set goals for the company and other, less pleasant but important conditions: conditions of termination, inheritance in the case of death, and so on. As I spent a few months on this, I can't claim that it was easy to reach agreement. But it's always more difficult to correct mistakes than to do things right initially. Everything would have been much easier if I'd had this bright idea when I first started doing business with my partners. Once we reached consensus on our functions, the next level was to learn how to begin operating this way.

Differences between co-owners are the biggest disruptions for a company. Employees can take advantage of these differences to their benefit, which drives the wedge between co-owners even deeper. If the differences are so significant that they cannot be settled in the best interests of the company, it may not be a bad option for one of the owners to leave. It is much worse for a company when for a long period of time its co-owners cannot agree as to which partner is in charge. In the very beginning of my career as a consultant, I consulted with the three co-owners of a company, none of whom wanted to take responsibility for setting goals and managing the others. As a result, the process of implementing the management tools took over two years instead of the usual eight months. I have never had a more difficult and time-consuming project.

Investing money in a company and providing it with the means for production is an important function of an owner. The majority of retailing and manufacturing companies cannot begin operations without an initial investment, and will require additional investment while in the process of growing. Rapid growth requires even more resources. As a rule, a manufacturing company cannot even double its annual revenues without acquiring additional funding, as its level of profits would simply not be sufficient to support this growth. There are almost no prominent companies that have managed to grow rapidly without attracting investors.

An investor should understand that by investing money in a company, he entrusts it to a person who has demonstrated an ability to manage the business. An investor never sets goals for the companies he invests in. But if he starts his own investment company, then he would be the goal setter for this business. Situations in which, over time, an investor begins to indicate a desire to manage the company usually do not end well. Also, if you ever want to attract an investor as a partner in your company, I advise you to do business only with professional investors, never with the owners of other companies. By investing money in your company, an owner of another business has a particular viewpoint: a business owner's viewpoint. Owners investing in other companies is a common mistake in Ukrainian businesses, which is caused by poor development of the investment industry and the inability of owners of companies to attract the right kind of investors. As a rule, investors who have their own businesses are risk-averse and expect the level of profitability to be no less than that in their own businesses. Sooner or later, they begin to interfere with the management of the company they've invested in, thereby destroying the power of the person who sets the goals. Professional investors have a completely different way of thinking. They are interested in the company remaining stable and want its capital to grow. They don't want to deal with starting a business, and thus they are more focused on supporting the person who sets the goals for the company.

The decision on whether or not to find an investor is always based on how these investments influence the speed of the company's growth and the implementation of its purpose. For example, imagine you started a successful restaurant that has developed good revenues, and now you want to open more. Without attracting investments, it would take you a year to open the second restaurant. However, with outside investments, you will be able to open three restaurants over that same period of time. If you decide to bring in an investor who will become a co-owner, remember that you need to sign an agreement on the distribution of the functions and responsibilities of the owners. It's better to agree on this in the very beginning rather than wasting efforts on resolving the differences after a few years.

In small- and medium-size businesses, it often occurs that co-owners are also company executives. For example, one is the CEO, another is the sales director, while yet another is the COO. When a small company has multiple owners, it's almost inevitable that the larger the company grows, the more difficulties such a situation will create. If co-owners don't understand and distinguish their functions and responsibilities as owners from their functions and responsibilities as executives, they create problems in the management of the company. Very often such a situation becomes apparent when the orders of the CEO are not executed by his executives, who are also owners. They use their *co-owner* position in the performance of their *executive* roles, thereby unconsciously destroying the company's management structure. In addition, this leads to a situation in which a hired manager will never be able to survive at the senior management level. As such, there will not be any professional growth path for talented employees in the company, and upon reaching their ceiling, talented employees will leave the company. In such situations, the company becomes unmanageable. It is torn apart by controversy, and its growth stops.

The only way to prevent this from occurring is to make sure that every partner knows his or her function as a co-owner, and as an executive. While performing their functions as executives, they must behave like regular, salaried employees. This is the reason why when Visotsky Consulting consults for companies with multiple owners, we make sure that all co-owners participate in the project. We never take on consulting projects with companies where there are disagreements between co-owners. In companies plagued by co-owner disagreements, the organizational changes that may be carried out as part of the consulting project contribute to further disagreements, and the company loses more than it gains. If there are disagreements between co-owners, it is important to settle them first, then engage in the improvement of the company with the help of a consulting firm.

It is very difficult, if not impossible, to reach an agreement when the personal goals of co-owners with respect to the business are different. One can have a personal goal of creating a thriving international company, while another can have a goal of doing a job she likes and being creative in a particular field. In 2007, this was the reason I had to sell my share of Geroldmaster to my partner. There was a crucial moment when, from my point of view, in order to expand it was necessary to open production facilities in Russia and Europe. At that point, domination in the Ukrainian market had already been achieved because the company controlled a significant market share there. At the time, there were no obstacles to conquering the Russian market. We could leave all of the most complicated technologies, like designing and die[32] manufacturing, in Kiev but locate duplication facilities in Moscow. That was when my partner hit the brakes and our mutual understanding cracked. I was so absorbed by the idea of expansion that I even wanted to buy out his share of the business. To be honest, without his creativity, the company would not have been able to fully realize its purpose. Only with time did I realize that the real reason for what had happened was the initial difference in our personal goals. My partner's goal was to express himself creatively. My goal was to create a truly successful, world-renowned company. During the time in which the company's operations did not exceed the limits of his personal goal, he performed his functions as a co-owner with full dedication and managed the process of product manufacturing and its improvement. But as the scale of the company began to outgrow this goal and create discomfort for him, it no longer suited him. In fact, his creativity was the initial basis of the company's purpose, and he obviously was the person who set the goals. He delegated this role to me while it aligned with his personal goal. Without understanding the nature of what was happening, I was happy to deceive myself, and considered myself as the person who set the goals for the company, not even thinking that initially the medals were his «thing.» When I figured out what was happening, I sold him my share of the company. Now we have a great relationship, and I have the utmost respect and admiration for his talent and his products.

The spouse and family members of the owner belong to a special category of co-owners. From time to time in consulting, we face a situation where the husband or wife of an owner, acting out of belief that he or she has a right to half of the spouse's property, begins to interfere with the management of the company. At the same time, this person usually doesn't take full responsibility for any of the functions, but tries to be in the driver's seat in some particular area. Despite a spouse's best intentions to help run the business, this individual's personal goals are rarely focused on the company's prosperity. In short, sooner or later, problems arise with any partner who does not have a duty level of motivation toward the business.

If you consider such a situation acceptable and your spouse has the appropriate level of competence, you need to provide him or her with

---

[32] A die is a specialized tool used to cut or shape material using a press.

precise functions and areas of responsibility. These can be functions related to those of an owner or the functions of a particular position in the company. I just want to warn you, if you love your spouse and enjoy your married life, think about whether it's worth bringing work issues into your relationship. You see, your mutual admiration and love will not necessarily benefit from the fact that you have to interact on business issues. Management of a company includes demands, performance of duties, and discipline. Can you really treat your spouse the same way as a hired employee? Will it improve your relationship? If you have any doubt, don't risk it. A good marital relationship is too valuable. It brings a lot of joy, pleasure, and inspiration to our lives — so don't spoil what works well!

Chapter 16

....

The Code of a Business Owner

Here are some rules I recommend be followed by the person who sets the goals for a company. These rules are the result of my observations of the most significant problems that arise in a business.

1. Live by Your Own Goals

Don't try to live like other people live. Society tries to impose its own standards in order for you to become easier to exploit. It convinces people how long they need to work, how long their vacations should be, how and where to spend their time, which entertainment to choose, which books to read, and which movies to watch.

The majority of people don't even think about the fact that by leading a «normal» life and doing the same things most people do, they'll get the results most people get. They dream about outstanding results but conduct their lives like everyone else without realizing that they will merely get average results.

You're not like everyone else, and an attempt to live a «usual» life will lead to disappointment. Everything you create in life for yourself, for your company, and for others is based on your personality, the basis of which is your goals. Your own goals are the starting point and a foundation, and your love for your goals is a source of inspiration and strength.

Appreciate your personal point of view and protect and defend it. Choose your own path and never be tempted to follow someone else's. The lives of many people depend upon your personal achievements. If you are full of enthusiasm and enjoy going forward on your own path, then your family, your employees, your customers, and the world will benefit from it.

2. Dream

Dreams are the first step toward creation. Anything that exists in the real world was first created in someone's dreams. The most beautiful things on this planet were created by people. The paradises dreamed up by people don't exist in nature. The closest things to paradise are luxurious and expensive resorts, which were created by people and are a materialization of their ideas. Wildlife fans will try to oppose me on this, but lush tropical forests where you constantly have to look around so that you don't step on a snake can hardly be called a paradise. The natural environment is a completely different thing, which is why it is referred to as «wild».

In society, dreamers are often criticized and teased, which is why smart people are quite careful about sharing their dreams. The destruction of any dream is the destruction of a piece of a probable future. It's difficult to completely destroy a material object. Even if it is burned or melted, something material will still remain. But a dream can be destroyed much faster, and without leaving any remains.

You, as the creator of a company and its products, are able to dream. So dream on a large scale. Write down all the good ideas that come to your mind. Dream about what is important to you and what truly inspires you. It absolutely does not matter what other people dream about. Create an environment in which you feel comfortable to dream, and then take the time to dream and make plans. Your dreams create a future for a lot of people.

3. Create a Facilitating Environment

You are surrounded by all kinds of people—business partners, employees, relatives, friends, and acquaintances. You chose some of them consciously, while others you may have received as part of a bundled deal[33]. Some of these people help and actively contribute to you and your ideas, some morally support you, some just criticize all of your ideas, and some obviously don't like you and criticize anything that has to do with you.

Sometimes you stay in contact with these toxic people just to keep up appearances. We are taught in childhood that it's important to be nice to people. However, what our elders neglect to mention is that we should not be nice to *all* people. I think that a kind attitude toward those who try to harm you is an obvious sign of behavioural inadequacy. The most talented people, those who want to achieve a lot and still enjoy life, choose their social network very carefully.

There is no reason to communicate with a person who is hostile toward you or your ideas. You don't have to communicate with hostile people, because nobody can obligate a person to destroy his own life.

---

[33] In the 1980s, in the USSR, the errors of the planned economy of the country led to a situation in which there was a shortage of some consumer goods while there was a surplus of others. In order to solve the problem, retail organizations sold items in demand only in sets with unmarketable surplus items as a «bundled» deal. For example, as part of a «bundled» deal for toilet paper, people were forced to buy soap as well.

That is why you should pay careful attention to who is around you and consciously create your network, especially since, unfortunately, there are plenty of people who like to spoil the mood of others and cause suffering. These people include both adults and children. At an airport recently, I saw a boy of about five years old who persistently and very deliberately bothered other children by trying to take away and break their toys and cause physical pain. When he was successful, I saw a sincere look of joy on his face. What a terrible scene! This boy will grow up and learn to hide his negative emotions. His inclinations won't change, but they will become less visible to others. It's not difficult to get to know the people around you. All you need to do is ask yourself, How do I feel after talking to this person?

The most common weapon used against you is the devaluing of your ideas. You say, «I came up with an idea on how to.» In response, you hear someone say, «It is impossible because.» Then you say, «We will do it this way.» And the reply is, «What makes you think you can do it?» Some of these people may be experts and seem very useful, but you can always weigh the benefits they bring with their knowledge against the harm they do to your goals.

Keep in contact with a person if he gives you strength and energy and if you feel more like your true self in his presence, and more confident in your talents and abilities. If you have more doubts, less desire to act, or suffer from fatigue and disappointment, then dismiss this person from your network. Don't waste your time on fools and destructive-minded people. This is not just a matter of your personal comfort; remember, too much depends on your state of mind.

4. Perform the Functions of a Leader

This is something no one can do for you. You can have brilliant salespeople, skilled managers, and experienced accountants, but you will not be able to hire a leader for your company. This is something you will have to do yourself until someday you finally retire from the business.

The reason you are a leader is because your creativity and courage inspire other people. Guide them to a victory and they will become stronger as they begin to believe in themselves, and their creativity will be revived. For this to happen, you need to keep in constant communication with your company's employees. If they do not know you and do not see you, the goals you promote will be significantly less real to them.

Usual routines and common problems will tend to distract your attention from performing the functions of a leader, but by addressing these less important problems and not dealing with the most important tasks, you will never be able to achieve your goals.

Reinforce your authority. Even though it is indivisible by nature, in order to reinforce your authority you need to delegate some of it to others. By passing a part of it to others, you remain its source. Do not let anyone take your authority away from you. Only you have the right to it and bear its responsibility, as you are the one who created the company. Anyone who attempts to destroy your authority destroys the company you created, regardless of whether he realizes it or not.

In order to maintain and reinforce your authority, create an elite group within your company. The elite group consists of those people who fully support you. Give them authority and privileges that symbolize their special status in the company. Look after them, be concerned about the quality of their lives, be engaged in their education and advancement, and make sure they fully understand your ideas about the company's growth. Large companies are not created by a single person. They are the result of a number of talented people's creativity.

5. Don't Be Gullible

Gullibility can sometimes be seen as innocence, but, in essence, it is irresponsibility. Rather than looking at issues and making a decision for himself, a gullible person passes the decision making and, in fact, his own destiny to someone else. Gullibility is not acceptable in a leader. By acting on an idea that he has not personally assessed, he is transferring responsibility and betraying the trust of those around him.

In the modern world, too many people who act as experts in some area present their opinions as facts. Read the reviews of your favorite books or movies and you'll see how strange the opinions of «experts» can be. Today it's become acceptable for people to discuss books they've never read, and teach something that they have never done themselves. This doesn't mean there are only false ideas around, but you can always weigh an idea against your personal experience and values in order to evaluate whether it makes sense. Observation of life allows to you to distinguish truth from falsehood.

I want to make special mention of mass media, especially television. In the process of the evolution of mass communications, TV people found that the easiest way to attract people's attention was to talk about problems, catastrophes, scandals, and celebrities. That is why they allocate so many resources to these topics. It's understandable, as there is very fierce competition in this arena. However, don't be fooled, as such «news» has almost no valuable information that can be used to your benefit. Personally, I haven't watched TV for more than ten years; I get my news from newspapers and the Internet. At least this way I can choose what to read, rather than being forced to swallow bundled news bites. When you read, as opposed to listening, it's much easier to verify and assess information. Television always adds a particular emotional slant to facts by skillfully manipulating images. With today's technology, an event or person can be shown from any angle. Even Mother Teresa can be made to seem a menace to viewers. These methods are used to promote certain ideas.

Thinking based on the opinions of recognized «authorities» allows you to be manipulated. Improve your ability to distinguish facts from opinions. Evaluate ideas by examining facts. The only final authority for you is you.

6. Be Careful About Money and Possessions

Be concerned about money as an important source of energy for yourself and your company, but do not set money making as a goal on its own. If you set money making as the goal, you can lose the most important thing that gives you your strength: your ideals. Money is too small a goal for anyone. Remember, you need much more than money! At the same time, control of money matters will help you not to get distracted by little things, and a good income will provide comfort and the opportunity to do what you consider most important for yourself.

When you possess many things, it can make you stronger, but it can also devour your creative energy. Personally, I cannot imagine my life without an assistant to help manage my household and maintain order there. If faced with the choice of having a more expensive house or an assistant, I would choose the latter. When you buy an expensive car or house, think about whether you can ensure that these things don't take up an excessive amount of your time and attention, but instead bring you pleasure. Among my friends, there are many who are forced to spend a significant amount of their time on improvements to their newly purchased homes. It doesn't occur to them that if they focused all of that time and energy on the growth of a company, they could have even better homes and perhaps pay for some help to maintain them. Assess any object you buy from the point of view of whether it will just divert your attention rather than satisfy a real need. If you aren't yet able to afford the cost of high-quality maintenance for a vacation home, which you will use for just a couple of months a year, perhaps for now it makes sense to get by with vacationing at luxurious resorts. If the purchase of an expensive car just causes you discomfort because of the need to maintain it, maybe for now you should purchase a less expensive car that can easily be serviced by a brand-name repair shop.

Don't kill your creativity by possessing too many things. Things can steal your attention and weaken your potential.

7. Increase Your Competence

If a person isn't competent in an area, she will inevitably make mistakes that will bring her disappointment—mainly disappointment in her own abilities. In fact, disappointment in your own abilities is the only thing that can substantially harm you.

Your courage and persistence will push you forward, but lack of competence in an area will multiply disappointments and lower your courage and persistence. You can easily retain your strength if you improve your competency in those areas where you are unable to get results, or where it is difficult for you to do something. Any activity can be difficult if you engage in it without having the necessary skills. Continuous improvement of your competence will allow you to retain your vitality and get significantly more pleasure from your victories.

Your competence as the business owner is the most valuable asset of your company, and it is worth investing time and money in. Furthermore, it is your most secure asset. We live in a world that is not entirely safe, but no one can take away from you your abilities and competence. Your education as an owner is more important than the education of your executives or the purchase of new equipment. In order to see just how important it is, think of how your company would look today if at the early stages of its operations you could have done everything you are capable of today.

Afterword

Recently, I was interviewed by the editor of one of the business magazines in Russia. After asking me questions about the role of a business owner, he added, «Among journalists, there's an opinion that your company is a cult that promotes the idea that business owners are special people who have special characteristics, and that you have created a cult of business owners. What do you say about this?» His question amused me and gave me something to consider. My reply was that I really do think all business owners are a special kind of people. In modern society, almost all valuables that define quality of life are created at the will of business owners. The largest components of human life are supplied by products created by entrepreneurs — food, clothing, entertainment, and different kinds of services. The technology we use in our lives and the goods people buy all depend on vision of the business owner.

The future doesn't get created by governments. Ideas for the future are conceived of by scientists and artists, but it is entrepreneurs who turn them into a specific purpose and bring them to life. Many things in society depend on how competently the business owner does his job.

For some strange reason, monuments to owners of outstanding companies are not erected, entrepreneurship museums are not created, and very rarely are business owners recognized by being presented with state awards. I think this is foolish and unfair, and I hope someday it will change. I dream that in the future there will be museums where everyone can see and understand how businesses are formed, and can look behind their facades to see how outstanding companies and their products were actually created.

In this book, I have written about only the most important functions of a business owner. Of course there are many other topics — about how to organize a company's operations, how to create a holding company, and how to apply management tools. These are topics for future books.

I would sincerely appreciate receiving your questions, reviews, and comments. Send them to alex@visotsky.org. Your inquiries will help me to write future books about the business owner's profession.

I wish you great goals and enjoyment of their achievement!

Made in the USA
Charleston, SC
04 February 2017